MYTHS OF CHOICE

why people won't change and what you can do about it

First published by Communicate31 Pty Ltd
Level 26, 44 Market Street, Sydney
NSW 2000, Australia
https://communicate31.com

This book is based upon the original publication: *The Myths of Life and the Choices We Have* (Clare Mann, 2005).

ISBN: 9780987346117

NATIONAL LIBRARY OF AUSTRALIA

A catalogue record for this book is available from the National Library of Australia

Dedication

To all the renegades, outliers and thought-leaders who refuse to blindly accept society's conditioning. To those individuals who are prepared to open-mindedly examine their own choices and open people up to collective myths. To those who recognise the myths that keep us locked in small-mindedness and social ways of being that masquerade as freedom, but are really forms of oppression, prejudice, and institutionalised socio-economic slavery.

To all the animals whose voices are not currently being heard because we choose not to hear them, and to everyone who advocates on their behalf to end speciesism and animal exploitation.

What People are Saying

Clare's brilliant and illuminating sequel to "Vystopia" delves into the fascinating psychology behind the intractable many of us are faced with and our own often, lives lived by default. Clare uses her life experiences to encourage you to do the same in identifying transformative life events. The eight myths she focuses on will allow you to face your fears, preconceived ideas and break free through practical exercises that will help liberate your life, enjoy better relationships and live your life to its greatest potential. This is a beautifully researched labour of love designed to help all of us reach our best self and in turn help others and all the glorious species we share this planet with. From wisdom and courage "Myths of Choice" will, if utilised, revolutionise your life.

Lynda Stoner
CEO Animal Liberation NSW

When you've had your eyes opened, woken up from the programming, and become vegan, you experience a seismic shift in your worldview. As Clare says in her book Vystopia, it's an existential crisis. Clare now delves deeper into why people so resist having their world view altered, and why they won't change despite knowing it is harming animals, people and planet. Through a journey of self-discovery, she provides tools to understand and break through people's resistance and get them to embrace change.

Jane Velez-Mitchell
Author, Journalist
JaneUnChained.com

In a world where more and more people feel increasingly trapped by perceived obligation and duty, Clare dispels the various debilitating myths which make many resistant to change and choosing more freedom. Guided by frequent examples of her own rich experiences, readers are encouraged to consider and apply the material presented from their own unique perspective, which is both enlightening and empowering.

Equipping people with tools and techniques to address any anxiety, uncertainty, resistance, criticism, or fear, Myths of Choice helps them confidently begin the process of change and gives them permission and encouragement to shine. If only this invaluable resource was available over a decade ago when we made significant life changes, we could have avoided many difficult and painful challenges.

Natasha & Luca "That Vegan Couple"
Social Media Influencers, Vegan Advocates
thatvegancouple.com

Clare has an uncanny ability to find the underlying patterns and behaviours in people, that she then uses to remove the barriers towards a more compassionate world. She now passes on this knowledge, breaking it down into actionable exercises to give us the tools to be able to communicate effectively with a traditional society stuck in their ways. Change starts with transformative conversations, and this book will no doubt help you to do just that.

Michael & Maša Ofei
The Minimalist Vegan

If you find people's resistance to change frustrating and would like to learn more about the psychology behind traditional thinking that keeps us enslaved, this book is for you. Myths of Choices is full of practical exercises and tools which I look forward to using in my activism as well as my personal life, to improve my communication skills and have a better understanding of the human psychology.

Asal Alamdari
Co-founder of Anonymous for the Voiceless.

By identifying eight myths that commonly shape our lives—such as the myth that we are not good enough as we are or the myth that we should follow a moral code decreed by others—Clare Mann has created a valuable roadmap to challenging assumptions and recognizing why others are so reluctant to embrace new ideas and behaviours. Only when we understand the psychology behind our choices can we open the eyes of others to injustice while also expanding our own options. This is a must-read for anyone who wants to change hearts and minds.

Mark Hawthorne
Author of Striking at the Roots: A Practical Guide to Animal Activism

Myths of Choice is the perfect companion to Clare Mann's seminal book, Vystopia. Once again, Clare has lifted the veil on why people behave the way they do — in this case why we resist change — and provides social justice advocates with simple yet powerful strategies to shatter the beliefs we hold about ourselves and our lives, and to help others do the same. The insights and tools she shares are a valuable gift to activists in their quest to create a kinder world.

Katrina Fox
Journalist, Author, Founder of Vegan Business Media

I eagerly awaited Vystopia's release and it was a timely, relevant soundtrack for my life as a vegan and animal rights activist last year. My interactions with people as a result have changed and when I feel angry and frustrated, I refer back to those learnings. Myths Of Choice is no different. Through understanding why we have our beliefs and foundations, it's up to us to challenge ourselves to dive past them and see if they are relevant to who we are. These myths, when put into one book, make it easier to understand why we feel the way we do and why so many people end up compromising themselves, and ultimately remain unsatisfied and unhappy. Only we can change how we see the world and how we feel. It starts with "me/us" not "them." Thank you for such an essential and frankly-written book.

Jason Alan
Sydney Animal Save

Clare Mann has a knack for identifying life's tough questions and providing realistic answers. When you have facts and logic on your side, but your dad at family dinner or an office colleague at after-work drinks are resistant to changing their views, your own language matters. Myths of Choice can help you in these tricky situations. Our times are crying out for urgent solutions. If you stand up for the environment, human rights, animal rights, and peace, this book is an important companion.

Lee Rhiannon
Former Senator, Australian Greens Party

Unlike any other book on change, Myths of Choice provides a much needed, deeper, and holistic understanding of the change process. As a Psychotherapist and Social Ecologist, I am delighted that this outstanding book also gives insight into how society unconsciously collaborates against individuals making and wanting change. I highly commend this book.

Tao de Haas
Psychotherapist, Social Ecologist, Author

Clare has created a thought provoking and practical guide that explores humanity's resistance to change. This book systematically shows us how we can disentangle from the trappings of unquestioned beliefs and habits, to live with more intention, authenticity, and accountability. This is an essential read for all activists, change agents, and social justice advocates!

Dr Ash Nayate
Neuropsychologist and author of
Staying Positive in a F*cked Up World

Clare outdoes herself in this book. I'm blown away by the accuracy and relevance. This is an essential read; I'm grateful for what I now understand about human psychology and communication.

Paul Bashir
Co-Founder and Director for Anonymous for the Voiceless

Clare Mann delivers another essential read for any social justice warrior or activist, with this thought-provoking and practical tool for positive change. This book wonderfully illustrates how activists, by managing their emotional and physical states, can become empowered to change themselves so they can be the best possible example and influence to others.

Mark Doneddu
Coordinator, World Vegan Day

Myths Of Choice makes for compelling and at times confronting reading. Clare Mann is an extraordinary author and expertly guides the reader through self examination to enable understanding of why others are reluctant to change behaviour/s. Highly recommended to those with open minds who want to open hearts.

Patty Mark
Animal Liberation Victoria

In Myths of Choice: Why People Won't Change and What You Can Do About It, psychologist and author Clare Mann challenges us to explore the big topics of life: Uncertainty. Fear. Morality. Social pressures. Selfishness. All to understand why people, ourselves, and those around us, believe what we do and why we hold on so tightly to those beliefs. In Myths of Choice, Ms. Mann gives us the tools to overcome life-limiting inertia in ourselves and others. She offers rich rewards through that effort: Authenticity. Courage. Happiness. Freedom! If you are ready for a life without limits, put Myths of Choice: Why People Won't Change and What You Can Do About It high on your "must read" list.

Michael Klaper, M.D.
Physician and Author

In today's world where we are facing environmental destruction, massive animal abuse, over population, gender inequality, financial exploitation and endemic political corruption, this powerful and accessible book helps us step back from ourselves to reassess our life's journey.

Dr Tracie O'Keefe DCH, BHSc, ND
Clinical hypnotherapist, psychotherapist and naturopath,
Australian Health & Education Centre
www.tracieokeefe.com & www.doctorok.com

Foreword

As a psychiatrist and animal activist, I'm privy to pain. Joyous, happy, pain-free people usually do not look for me — so everyday I am flooded with sad narratives. No surprise!

What is astonishing, however, is the epidemic of existential angst I hear about daily in towns across America. Statements like, 'What's the point? Working my whole life — and then I kick the bucket!'

After Clare Mann invited me to write this foreword, I found Victor Frankl's book researched the term "existential angst." Here is what I found.

In Man's Search for Meaning, Victor Frankl characterised the American culture as suffering from Existential Hunger, or the condition called an 'existential vacuum' in which a person doubts their life has meaning. Widespread in the twentieth century, the vague symptoms were described as a loss of interest in life. Frankl hypothesised it was related to the advent of industrialisation, with the waning of animal instincts and social traditions leaving people without direction or initiative. As a group, seeking conformity over individualism and needing to depend on others, they neglected their own personal lives. Life was empty — a huge hole could never be filled. Such a sad picture! This reminds me of the composite portrait in Clare's book; a patient burdened by all seven myths, and she's itching to change.

Next I began reading Clare Mann's masterful book: Myths of Choice: why people won't change and what you can do about it. Clare co-partners with the reader as she gently takes you through 50 written practices, asking questions about your life, values, emotions, beliefs, and myths that are influencing you in your life. Enjoy this in-depth process of inquiry. I went ahead and did some research on myths because I was definitely rusty in the myth department.

I discovered that myths are complex social and cultural influences, not just symbolic and certainly not true. Rather, myths are beliefs based on our own personal values and experiences that give meaning to our lives. Meaning grounds us, providing a base to jump from and fly to even greater heights in life. Without meaning we are simply lost and disoriented with anxiety creeping up. In existentialism, myths help us to understand our human condition, enabling us to deal with the 'givens' of life (freedom, death, isolation, and meaning).

Myths can become a big problem, especially if they are believed as factual or considered dogma. We need to question our myths and their meaning regularly, making sure they still fit and bring us positive benefits. Clare does an exquisite job in helping you re-evaluate them. In the text, she debunks seven myths to effect changes and healing, transforming stuck situations that are resistant at first to change. There may come a time where a myth is no longer viewed as a myth, but as a factual truth, and that's when the problems begin.

As an existential psychologist, Clare explores the reasons people resist making changes. She challenges the reader to identify their unconscious social myths that limit choices, constrict life, and extinguish freedom. The good news: you are already free! Jean-Paul Sartre said so in 1943 when he wrote that humans are 'condemned to be free.' How awesome is that? So why is change so difficult for people?

People fear change — it's natural for us humans! Even the thought of change can trigger a fear response. What's interesting is that people fear being labeled as 'the outsider,' and dread no longer fitting into their 'comfortable' culture or social groups. Change feels unsafe and threatening to a person's identity since their worldview is about to change soon. This fear intensifies when family and friends lack insight. By understanding myths, interwoven in people's psyche, now you can help a patient, friend, or social justice movement in moving your message with boldness and greater efficacy. It's not trickery! It's about coming to terms with conscious and unconscious choices, and realising how people live in a perennial trance; a state of assuming, which is not freely chosen because it is moulded by myths.

Myths help you to understand change and its complexities, based on culturally shared assumptions, and especially in relation to a person's identity and sense of belonging. Messy dynamics! Existential therapy explores our human condition — questions about life and death: Who am I? What is my purpose? Is there a God? What happens when you die?

Before dealing with big questions like these, Clare helps you to first understand your own emotions and delicately guides you step-by-step, gradually and methodically, in a non-judgmental way. She is an excellent role model as an extraordinarily compassionate human. A great balance of strength and compassion through a well-planned enquiry process. Most people need a great guide or teacher who can help them to navigate the emotional terrain of paradoxical questions — she is a wise therapist.

I wish you well in entering Clare's world, and more importantly, in discovering your own mind and body, heart and relationships, perhaps in new and fearless ways. I found courage in Clare's words, and wisdom in her style of counselling. In lifting the veils of denial, endemic in our culture, you can explore the paradox of our human condition: a species capable of immense love and sensitivity but also, immense hatred, brutality, murder and wars. Through self-inquiry, your eyes open wider, crafted mindfully by yourself. Thank you Clare, for opening my eyes.

Marilyn Kroplick, MD,
Psychiatrist and President of In Defense of Animals

Acknowledgements

The seeds of a new book are planted years, if not decades, before the writer puts pen to paper. These seeds are incubated and when their time and conditions are right, they sprout and give signs of what they may look like when nurtured, fed and helped to grow to maturity. This book is no exception and it's impossible to name all the people or experiences that have contributed to the final version.

Thank you to my parents, Victor and Gabriel Mann who encouraged me to ask bigger questions and asking what we're here for. To my nan Lillian Mary Rose who taught me to look for the rainbow, my grandmother Tilly Ashton who broke with convention and started a career in London in her fifties in the 1960s. Thank you to all my teachers along the way including: Harry Browne, Buckminster Fuller, Greg Braddon, Edward Snowden, Joe Dispenza, and that taxi driver in Israel whose name I never heard and who reminded me that sometimes freedom can be a form of mental slavery. Thank you to Barbara Streisand who, in the movie *The Way We Were*, inspired me to be that street activist and speak out for what is right, even when the majority ridicule and criticise.

Special thanks to everyone involved in bringing this book to fruition. To Marilyn Kroplik of In Defense of Animals for writing the foreword, Katrina Fox of Vegan Business Media for her strategic advice, Nadia Perry for the cover, Mem Davis for editing, re-writing, and reminders to take breaks. Of course, my thanks and respect for my partner and best friend, Brendan Norris, for questioning absolutely everything and reminding me that, 'No means not yet.' To my four legged family members Minka, Cosmo and Comet, and to Dasein and Topaz who will forever reside in my heart.

Contents

Preface

Having worked as an organisational psychologist for many years and later, training as an existential psychotherapist, I am intrigued as to what motivates people to change their behaviour. More importantly, why don't people change despite, in many cases, overwhelming evidence that it would not only benefit themselves and their families but their community, society and planet – especially with the latter crucial for their existence? Also, why do they espouse one thing and yet their current behaviour contradicts it?

History reminds us that social change occurs gradually, and then something happens that causes us to sit up and pay attention. For instance, awareness of environmental destruction, a health crisis, or a social injustice that results in people protesting to make others aware of what has been hidden. The status quo continues to exist only because people are either content with their choices or never question them. These choices are sometimes so embedded in their psyche, they don't even consider them a choice, for example, having a job, eating animals, or adopting the benefits of modern convenience despite the hidden cost to people and planet.

So, when people concerned about some form of social injustice speak out and organise themselves, they invariably meet with resistance from the majority who don't want to change or even think that there's a question to be asked. Resistance can be in the form of ridicule, criticism or outright verbal or physical violence. It is precisely at this point the issues are pushed onto the table and dialogue is had through media, celebrities, and key leaders.

At an individual level, people who speak out struggle with the resistance they get from family, friends and work colleagues, especially when it's so obviously an injustice and other's choices are causing immense suffering to themselves, others or the planet. Examples include telling people about health issues associated with smoking, excessive alcohol consumption or the use of plastics bags. Why do people either ignore the message or attack the messenger?

From an existential perspective, resistance to change is normal and predictable. Human beings avoid uncertainty. Not the uncertainly as to what will happen tomorrow, but rather a fundamental shift in how they experience themselves, other people, and the world at large. Look around at such attempts to avoid and make the world predictable by adhering to fixed beliefs around things such as family, career, countries, parenting, sexuality. Most people believe that these are underpinned by some notion of consensual reality, although each of these are experienced subjectively.

All experiences are subjective, but we try to make them objective and when things happen to challenge this, we are thrown into anxiety. For example, divorce when you believe marriage is forever, or government corruption when you believe politics is there for the people. The anxiety occurs because if this could happen, what else could happen? In those moments, we are forced to entertain the predictable nature of uncertainty. For some, it is so uncomfortable that they resist, instead bemoaning their bad luck or other's behaviour, rather than examining other things in their lives that might benefit from the reality that change is even possible.

'Myths' is the name I give to these unquestioned assumptions of how we should, ought and must be. Myths are socially and culturally created and maintained in order for us to see ourselves and the world as predictable.

They prevent us from taking full responsibility for how we want to be or could be, as implied by phrases like, 'I could never do that.' This is why so many people stay in jobs or relationships that cause them so much misery. Not believing that we have a choice is called Choice Denial.

When a social injustice or environmental catastrophe is brought to light by a growing group of passionate people, resistance is normal. When resistance to even examining the issues is out of proportion to the threat imposed by changing, it is indicating the avoidance of existential uncertainty.

This book is written for anyone who wants to understand the psychology of why people resist change and what you can do to break the impasse. It's for those who are frustrated and bewildered as to why people won't make better choices, when their current ones cause so much suffering to people, animals and planet. The best way to examine this is to use yourself as a test subject, and see what unquestioned assumptions you hold and how to break through them to become more open-minded and amenable to change. You can then use this experience to help others make changes that will benefit us all.

Chapter 1

Dispelling the Myths

Despite the vast number of options of how we can live our lives, there is enormous similarity in what the majority do. In capitalist economies, the stereotype is to work for someone else, strive to buy your own home, believe you must get ahead and so go to college, get married, have children, invest in a retirement fund, travel, and so on and so forth. Have you ever wondered why there is so little variation from the norm and why so many people, despite not being fulfilled, refuse to change or even believe it is possible?

People resist changing. When a social movement implores people to change, it comprises individuals deciding to change for a reason far greater than living with the status quo, even if such change is resisted by family, friends and sometimes society as a whole. Some examples include:

- Veganism
- Minimalism
- Gender Equality
- Nomadic Living
- Child-free families
- Selling up and travelling, post-retirement

Many books exist on the nature of societal change and social movements. That is not what this book is about. Instead, it takes a step back and looks at the context within which individuals make choices, or, as we shall see, deny they have any choice or can't see those available. It focuses on understanding the inner world of other people and their avoidance (often unconscious or unquestioned) of existential uncertainty. Existential philosophy is complex and the principles are often hard to grasp, but myths enable us to understand it more easily as it is applicable to our own and other people's lives. This then creates a roadmap with which to understand why others won't change when faced with a social justice issue which has implications for everyone.

Personal Change

I want you to embrace personal change and mastery in your own life.

Personal change and mastery in my own life began with challenging these alleged choices and questioning ways in which I could really exercise freedom in my life. It involved developing a very personal relationship with myself and trusting that I was the best judge of what was good for me. It required me to challenge others' expectations, and appreciate the ways in which I was created and defined by what I did and with whom I interacted. It invited me to question what I wanted from my life and the unchallenged assumptions under which I operated. It allowed me to evaluate the rightness of my choices rather than using other people's criteria of success. This way of being became a journey, not a destination.

Numerous suggestions have been offered of how to bring about change in our lives. Some operate as a self-help checklist, where goals and objectives are set to focus the reader on realising their potential. Others offer a way to escape from the daily treadmill and become more independent and autonomous in our work. However, real freedom to exercise the choices in our lives comes from recognising that we already have complete freedom now to be who we want to be. Slavish adherence to goal-setting and planning can become as much a trap as going along with what is expected of us by others.

So often people say, 'I would like to do something different but I can't because of my family, my job, my responsibilities.' When they say this they are making a choice – the choice that it is better to stay where they are than to change. The reason they don't change is not because of the family, job or responsibilities, but the choice they make to continue that lifestyle.

Often major life events initiate change in our lives: the death of a family member, loss of a job, divorce, or illness. Sometimes we are suddenly plunged into the depths of fear and despair, which results in us becoming paralysed and desperately wanting to maintain the status quo. Alternatively, we may embrace the change and make new choices that alter our lives even further. Why do we so often rely on imposed change to make those choices? How can we harness the energy and power to choose desirable changes as a way of being in the world? If we fail to embrace change, our life will become like the wallpaper in our home – at first we notice its pattern and texture, but after a time we cease to realise it is there. We also need to know what to change and what not to. Change for change's sake is as meaningless or as constraining as not exercising choices. Everything we do in life can be done with passion and direction rather than duty and obligation.

So, how can we realise those choices and make the changes in our lives that we want? I believe that insight begins with identifying the underlying assumptions and values we have about ourselves and others which inform our life and may limit the choices we believe are available to us. Our values underpin everything we do, and when these are challenged or when we place ourselves in situations that compromise those values, we often feel defeated or powerless. We may resort to blaming others for our predicament and focus on how to improve our interactions and communication with others. This rarely works because we are no longer working from a strong internal base. We have compromised our own values and lowered the value we put on ourselves. Communication and relationships can only improve if we honour our values and operate from a position of autonomy and freedom. Therefore, we need to get in touch with what is important to us – our own values – and then see how they inform our lives.

Some of our values are so strongly held that they immediately come to mind; others may be inferred from our behaviour and life choices to date. In order to identify them it is helpful to begin with a review of your life and the choices you have made to date. You can then gauge their value so far and make more informed choices about their meaning in your life today.

Critical Incidents in Your Life

Instead of writing down a list of activities in chronological order, it is useful to identify the critical incidents in your life that have been important. In experiencing your life today, events, feelings, dreams, perceptions and expectations from various points in the past inform this experience. You may look back and pinpoint certain chronological events, but your experience of being in the world now is informed by numerous influences which have not necessarily occurred chronologically. Critical incidents are memorable and influence key factors that inform your life now. They may even be experienced as your identity; 'me' in some sense, as they provide the basis for your personal history.

Every day we have a multitude of experiences, some of which appear to reflect the routine nature of our lives, while others stand out as important or memorable. For instance, we tend to remember key events like our first day at school, our graduation, the day we became vegan or did a parachute jump. A good example of the memorable nature of critical incidents is to ask yourself, 'What was I doing on September 11th when the Twin Towers in New York were attacked?' or, 'When Donald Trump was elected President of the United States?' Many people remember where they were, who they were with and what they were doing. However, if you ask yourself,

'What did I do two weeks ago last Tuesday?,' unless it was a key date in your diary, you will have difficulty remembering. The same thing happens when we reflect on our life journey so far.

Exercise 1

Imagine you were asked to give a pen picture of some critical events or things that have influenced your life direction. What would you include? They may be a conversation with a stranger on the train, solo travelling, or a sudden and unexpected turn of events. The experience made you feel you had really learnt something or left you feeling completely different. Write down the key events that you feel have influenced your life.

Example

About fifteen years ago, I lived in a rural area of New Zealand. I thought my partner and I had found paradise, and a particular experience sowed the seeds for a massive change in my life. One night I heard the unrelenting howling of dogs from the next property. My partner and I investigated only to find five dogs in outdoor cages, brutally thrown in there and covered in blood and cuts. One of them had been scored by a wild pig and I learnt later that they were part of pig-dogging, a barbaric practice where dogs are starved for up to four days, and then taken out to hunt pigs. Demented with hunger, they viciously tear pigs to death for the hunters, who see this as sport, to retrieve. The next day I got the SPCA to investigate. They took the dogs away, only to be returned as the hunters tidied up the cages, promising to treat them better.

This, and another experience of witnessing calves being brutally taken from their mothers within the first week of birth (so the dairy industry could sell the colostrum and milk), made me ask more questions. Hearing that herd of mother cows bellow and cry for thirty hours without stopping, then all stop at once in a piercing silence, made me ask more questions. Upon our return to Australia, my partner researched industrialised animal use and after watching videos, we and our two dogs became vegan on the spot.

What did I learn from that experience? I couldn't believe that my ethical choice to be a vegetarian for the past thirty years was meaningless if I had wanted to avoid harming animals. How could I not see how the government, industrialists and marketers work very hard to keep that information from us? I couldn't believe that I was so naïve to believe that somehow milk and eggs were bi-products, instead of the incarceration of animals who suffer mercilessly in the system. The suffering imposed on animals through the dairy and egg industries is immense, and I felt lied to. I'd believed I was being ethical but realised that the only way to align my desire to cause as little harm to animals as possible was to become vegan.

The next two exercises invite you to explore some of those critical incidents. After these exercises, I offer you an example of a major event that shaped change in my life.

Exercise 2

Now take each of the events you wrote about individually and write as much as you can about them. Who was involved? What happened? Where were you? What was it about the event that made it so memorable? What did you learn in the situation? What happened to you as a result of this event?

Look back over the events you have identified as being critical to your life journey. You may wonder how these events have become lodged in your memory in such a way that they seem to make up who you are? However, they are not really you unless you see yourself as no more than a history of events or experiences. But they are important and shape the way you see yourself and what you tell others about yourself.

Exercise 3

Individually, take each of the events that you identified in Exercise 1. (My own example included only one event.) Ask yourself, 'What does this memorable event indicate in terms of what is important to me?' This will indicate something about your values. Begin your answers with: 'This was important to me because...'

Example

Becoming vegan challenged my existing value system. It showed me that if I wanted to avoid harming animals through my consumer choices and lifestyle, I had to become vegan. I also had to be part of the solution and become more active in telling others how they too have been lied to, and finding out meant they could make informed choices about their own lives.

Those two experiences in New Zealand sowed the seeds for me becoming a vegan, learning that:

- Uninformed choices are limited choices
- Never assume things but ask more questions
- Constantly ask, 'What else don't I know?'
- Peace of mind results when actions are aligned with values
- I want to be part of the solution and not part of the problem
- My suffering in life is minuscule next to that of animals
- It made me question what I wanted to do with the rest of my life

Have you ever wondered who you are and were in those situations? Who is the someone you recognise as yourself, regardless of situation, age, status, relationships? Who is the silent observer who is now recalling the events? Who was the observer then? This is a theme we will return to, but for now I want you to look at the events you described in Exercises 1 and 2 again and carry out the following exercise.

The answers you provide to these exercises will highlight some very important values in your life. So often we embrace changes at an earlier time in our lives, when we perceive that we have the freedom and time to learn new things. Then, as we make life choices, a sense of safety or duty inhibits our willingness to embrace new possibilities. For example, you may choose a career path or domestic arrangement and become successful at it. You achieve earlier set goals and establish a sense of mastery over your life. However, whilst there is a sense of mastery and safety in maintaining the status quo, you can become stifled and laden down with routine and duty. To consider changing your job or life situation becomes too threatening. Who would I be without my job? My current relationship? My status? What would happen if I no longer earnt the income I have worked so hard to secure? Instead of feeling safe and strong, you feel stifled, resentful, or just plain bored. You lack the energy to make changes and learn new things.

When this happens, you may try several strategies to reclaim that sense of rightness in your decisions. In Western society, organisations play on this need by reinforcing workers who invest excessively long hours in their work. You may work harder, spend harder, buy more material goods as markers of your success, and make your life so full that you no longer question your happiness. You forget what it is that makes you tick and gives you the sense of freedom and mastery over your life.

I mentioned at the beginning that we have complete freedom over who we want to be. I can hear you saying, 'But we don't – I couldn't just walk away from my family, my child, my job, my aged parent, my mortgage...' Yes you can – it is a Myth that you can't. I do not deny that these choices would cause certain anxiety and in many cases, pain and loss, but the fact remains that it is possible. It may not happen, nor may it be desirable, but the crux of freedom is realising that you are the captain of your mind and are free to think in whatever way you want. That is what freedom means. You may not have the financial resources to quit your job and follow your passion right now, or the good health to climb a mountain, but you are free to challenge the way you think about things. What is not true is that you have to do certain things because someone else decrees it. You don't have to follow a particular career path, buy a big house, be nice to your in-laws or attend family events unless you really want to. If you do these, it is because you choose to do them. Even if they feel like obligations, they are still choices. What I ask you to do is challenge your choices and appreciate that you can have control over your life. You can choose how you want to live your life and feel the thrill of exercising those choices.

Stifling our freedom begins with the very family into which we are born. From a young age we are taught that certain behaviour is acceptable and that other kinds of behaviour are not. Obviously a certain amount of socialisation is essential to allow us to operate in the world. Learning to respect and consider others, not causing people unnecessary pain or harm, and taking responsibility for our actions is essential if we are to engage meaningfully with others. However, numerous values which stifle our freedom can be imposed on us and often remain with us throughout our lives. They become so ingrained that we cease to question their validity. For example, we take for granted that it is normal to follow a certain career path, get married, create financial security, have children, and tolerate others we prefer not to spend our time with. I don't deny that many of those choices may bring pleasure to many people. But how carefully are they chosen? To what extent are they mere responses to a perceived limited set of choices? Only you can answer this. It is a Myth that we must choose from such a narrow range of options. If we do, instead of choosing the life we want to live, we become bogged down with obligation and duty – sometimes without even realising it.

Those key events you identified earlier that influenced you appear to no longer arise as you limit your horizons. Society then reinforces those obligations through schooling, work, media and culture. There are certain cultural expectations for many behaviours: how to dress, behave in public, be a mother, be the ideal partner, be a loyal employee. We may feel that we have mastery over our lives, but in fact we often exercise those choices within very clearly defined limits of what is acceptable. That isn't freedom. Anyone who resists family and societal pressures is seen as irresponsible or selfish. Vegans, for example, are labelled as 'preachy' or telling people what to do. We end up actively resisting any challenge to our current choices because the implications of such are just too scary. We believe that the values underpinning our behaviour are those we chose rather than those which have been imposed on us.

I want you to challenge these obligations and duties and question the rightness of them. This will inevitably cause anxiety, since it questions assumptions in your life which you probably now take for granted. As the existential writer Rollo May says:

> *When we are called upon to do something new, to confront a no-man's-land, to push into a forest where there are no well-worn paths and from which no-one has returned to guide us, we will experience anxiety. This is what the existentialists call 'the anxiety of nothingness.' To live into the future means to leap into the unknown, and this requires a degree of courage*

> *for which there is no immediate precedent and which few people realise.*[1]

'Myths' is the label I give to the pressures to conform to the accepted behaviour of the majority. There are many Myths, which I believe influence and inhibit our decision-making and rob us of the freedom to choose our own way of being. I have chosen eight Myths and the following chapters will identify them. By working through the accompanying exercises, you will challenge their existence and value in your life.

Choosing a New Way of Thinking

Embracing your freedom requires new ways of thinking. This forms the philosophical basis on which choice and freedom can be realised. This new way of thinking requires you to:

- Challenge the assumptions under which you live your life,
- Evaluate the rightness of your choices according to your own criteria. Do not use others' criteria of success to judge them,
- Recognise that you have complete freedom to be who you want to be and to live the life you want to live,
- Identify the values which inform your life choices and question the rightness of them,
- Value your uniqueness and appreciate that you are the best judge of what is right for you,
- Appreciate that you are the captain of your own mind and that you are free to think about things in any way you choose.

Chapter 2

The Identity Myth

You're not good enough as you are, or, fitting in with others' expectations will bring you happiness.

The Nature–Nurture Debate Revised?

The premise of Sartre's philosophy that Existence precedes Essence highlights our freedom to create ourselves as we would like to be, rather than that prescribed through our genes or circumstances. The anxiety resulting from the enormity of our freedom causes us to fool ourselves that we are not free, that objective reality exists and that we are fixed and certain – we live in Bad Faith.

Bad Faith is our attempt to create structures, beliefs, behaviours to hoodwink ourselves that we are not free to create our reality. Instead, the rules, norms, beliefs we experience are mere creations and not fixed for all time.

The cost of denying our freedom and falling prey to living our lives according to some objective rightness leads to more anxiety, as we live second-hand lives, dictated by the demands of others. Instead, we can embrace our choices and create who we want to be despite the anxiety that meaningful living entails.

We are born into families, institutions and cultures that have expectations of us from the moment of birth. Many parents wish for their children all the things that they never had for themselves. They don't stop to wonder whether the child really wants these things. In reality, because of their own socialisation, they probably don't even question this themselves.

By the time the child is old enough to reflect on their parents' influence, they have already been socialised into valuing certain things in certain ways. Thus, limits have already been placed on their available choices.

The late R.D. Laing, a psychiatrist and author, offered original and unorthodox ways of considering mental health and illness. His ideas extended to society and the limits it imposes on how we experience our lives. He more forcibly expresses the view that limits are placed on our choices from birth by saying:

> *From the moment of birth, when the stone-age baby confronts the twentieth-century mother, the baby is subjected to forces of outrageous violence, called love, as its mother and father have been, and their parents and their parents etc., mainly concerned with destroying most of its potentialities. This enterprise is on the whole successful. By the time the new human being is 15 or so, we are left with a being like ourselves. A half-crazed creature, more or less adjusted to a mad world. This is normality in our present age.*[2]

Whilst Laing's views are considered by many to be extreme, the basic tenet of his beliefs does highlight the notion that our freedom is limited by social and cultural Myths. We frequently observe others when deciding how to live our lives, how to dress, how to spend our leisure time, how many hours to work or whether or not to have children. We behave stereotypically and allow fashion and general consensus to dictate the direction of our lives.

The modern scientific perspective reinforces this tendency. Psychologists and sociologists study large samples of behaviour and then tell us what is 'normal.' Most large businesses now use psychometric performance measures to predict an employee's future behaviour. Although trained as a psychologist, I am often bewildered at the extent to which faith is put in this method. I sometimes find it difficult to predict my own behaviour, let alone that of someone whom I have never met! And yet, there is a tremendous desire to make generalisations and find out what is measurable, predictable, acceptable and 'normal.'

Statistics

Scientific prediction of performance at work is big business as test providers try to measure, compare, and predict our behaviour. Some organisations only make job offers with supporting psychological profiles. The media also welcomes measurement and comparison – magazines and books offer ways to analyse our own behaviour, personality type and how to choose a suitable partner based on some generalised patterns of being. Whether it is predicting someone's emotional intelligence at work or their style of relating to the opposite sex, such measures diminish our individuality and reinforce the belief that we are merely part of a bigger group of which there is a limited number of measurable ways of being.

This is not the whole story. Tests may, by using statistical techniques, show relationships between different variables but in doing so they destroy the richness and complexity of people as individual and unique identities. The Identity Myth is one which hoodwinks us into believing that we should constantly measure ourselves against others to ensure we are normal.

Remember, you are a unique work in progress. No one has ever lived your life, thought your thoughts, walked in your shoes or lived your personal story. Why then allow statistics and other people's behaviour to dictate your life direction? The Identity Myth simply says that it is desirable to be like others, regardless of whether your inner needs, desires or voice suggest otherwise.

Take, for example, the number of hours that people choose to spend in the office. In many western countries, despite legislation limiting working hours, large numbers of people continue to work long hours in excess of the required amount. You then hear them saying, 'I have that Monday morning feeling' or 'Let's finish early – it is Friday after all.' This seemingly indicates that people are working against their real desires but is often laughed off as normal, acceptable and, in many cases, desirable.

No one can make you spend more time in the office unless you truly want to! It is possible for you to stand up, take your coat and say goodnight at a reasonable hour. But what stops us from doing this? The Identity Myth! The Myth that we must be like everyone else if we are to be normal, accepted and not stand out from the crowd. Many people say, 'But jobs are scarce and if I leave on time my job will be on the line.' Do you really want to work in an environment where fear and threat are the key motivating forces? Others convince themselves that they are committed to prevailing organisational ideals and that they enjoy the process. Many do. They may feel they belong or are valued, but they still make jokes about leaving early on Friday afternoons.

Could it be that we no longer look further than socially acceptable ideals to make our life choices? Could it be that we have to bend ourselves into certain shapes to justify what is really a Myth? Clearly, many people enjoy their work or aspects of it. However, I challenge you to evaluate the extent to which you are 100% committed to your current life choices, in particular, your work.

You may find it difficult to identify something in your life that you do with 100% commitment. Maybe it has been too long since you really did choose to do something that you wanted to. You may recognise your life as no more than a series of commitments and duties. If this is so, do not become disheartened. Change is always possible and by working through the exercises in this book, you will begin to see that the life you are leading now is a choice, and one that can be changed.

Exercise 4

Think of something you do that you can honestly say isn't done with 100% commitment and choice. It may be something you do at work or at home. It may be visiting relatives or shopping with your spouse or drinking with work colleagues on a Friday night.

- Write as much detail as possible: how often you do it, how long it takes, how long you have been doing it.
- What are the actual benefits of doing it?
- Now write the reasons you give yourself and others for doing it.
- Outline the actual cost of continuing to do it. This can be expressed in financial terms but also in emotional, health or psychological terms.
- What would happen if you no longer did it?
- What are the real reasons that you continue to do it?

If you were able to answer Exercise 4, it may have brought up some reactions and feelings. The answer to the last question is often the most telling. Once you have outlined how often you do something, the pros and cons of continuing it and the consequences of no longer doing the things you don't want to do, the real reasons for doing it change. Often people use words like 'should,' 'must,' and 'ought' in their answers. Such words echo elements of the Identity Myth – we must do something because someone else expects it, it is our duty, other people do it so that's what is expected. Once we get in touch with the real reasons, we find it is not because we fear others' reactions. It stems from a desire to reduce the anxiety that comes from saying 'no' to someone else, or daring to be different at the expense of being called abnormal or selfish.

However, our inability to trust our own knowing and do what is best for us results in a life that is not the one we want to lead. Other problems arise. We lose our ability to judge what is right for us. We stay late in the office because it is expected, because others do it; we feel alienated and different if we don't follow the crowd; we are unable to separate ourselves from stereotypical expectations of our role requirements. We also believe that if we are feeling stifled or pressured, this is normal because others are feeling so too. Thus we relinquish our power by looking to others as to what is appropriate and in the meantime our precious life is passing us by. We stay in jobs we don't like because that is what is expected. We stay with partners who make us unhappy because we assume that this is the way all relationships end up. It just isn't so – it is the Identity Myth.

Rollo May has written widely on the search for personal fulfilment and growth. He highlights the importance of being true to your own self when he says:

> *...if you do not express your own original ideas, if you do not listen to your own being, you will have betrayed yourself. Also you will have betrayed your community in failing to make your contribution to the whole.*[3]

In 'making a contribution to the whole,' May does not mean going along with the expectations of the majority. He is using this term in the same way as Jean-Paul Sartre, the existential writer and novelist, who maintains that we are totally free to create who we want to be. He says that the choices we make do impact on others, for in choosing our life direction, we are silently stating the way we believe it should be for others. For example, if we decide to follow a particular religion we are making a statement of how we believe it should be for others: that holding particular religious convictions is desirable, merely because we have acted in this way.

Another element of the Identity Myth is that we expect others to feel and act as we do – they must, because the same expectations and pressures influence them. However this is not the case. Many will, but not always, and often unpredictably.

Let us consider a stereotypical example. Imagine a mother who observes her adult son working undesirably long hours or repeatedly drinking with colleagues he finds boring. She may extend her understanding of his values and behaviour to other situations. She may expect him to behave in typical son manner – when he turns down the traditional Sunday lunch, she questions his love and commitment and feels short-changed. She correspondingly interprets his behaviour as not loving her – this must be so because that's what it means to other mothers.

Exercise 5

Jot down some of the events that have happened in your life where someone else's non-conformity to a given social expectation has upset you or made you feel unrecognised, unloved or unimportant. Make this personal, such as forgetting an anniversary. Write down as much information as possible in terms of:

- Who was involved?
- What happened?
- What was your response?
- What were your thoughts and feelings at the time?
- What are your thoughts and feelings now?

Look at your answers to this exercise. Typical examples include forgetting birthdays or not attending a work function. Your response may have been to become angry, withdrawn, sulky or aggressively indifferent. Your typical thoughts or feelings may be:

- I can't believe he expects me to stay home after having children – is this something out of the dark ages?

- Has anyone ever heard of a man who can't mend things around the house?
- How could she be so selfish? She knows that partners are expected to attend my work functions?
- I went to my daughter-in-law's house and she didn't even ask me to stay for dinner – what sort of wife is she to my son?
- He didn't buy me a Valentine's Day card – how could he be so selfish and unthoughtful?

Look at these and your own responses. Do you see anything in common? These responses are firmly based on the underlying belief that there are set ways of behaving, showing our love, expressing our needs or demonstrating our abilities. In allowing stereotypical patterns to dictate how we make sense of our lives and relationships, we are setting ourselves up for disappointment. By not accepting other people's uniqueness, we fall into the trap of making judgements. These are often misplaced and lead to changes in our behaviour, which result in us losing the very things we desire in the first place. The partner who is resented for forgetting Valentine's Day becomes tired and leaves, the judgemental mother-in-law doesn't see her family as much as she could, and the person who looks no further than norms to interpret others' behaviour becomes more confused and resentful. They might then say, 'This is how it must be.' This is the Myth. However, it becomes reality because we make it reality. We do not see reality as it is; we see reality as we are!

In order to choose the life you want to live, you must relinquish the notion that you can control others. You may feel that you control them by virtue of them responding to your demands, but invariably the time comes when they choose to do something else. You also lose your real power by focusing on changing other people rather than expending energy doing what you really want to do. This energy is better used attracting others with whom you are compatible into your life.

So often we lose faith in our own knowing and look for more and more information to interpret a certain situation or event. The underpinning belief is that if we can access sufficient information, an objective decision could be made. However, at any one time with exactly the same information, we are interpreting things in our unique way. Why then look for the 'right' way to do things from another's perspective? Surely this is self-defeating, since what is right for someone else won't be 100% right for you.

Exercise 6

Think of a time when you made a decision that, in hindsight, you would have made differently. For example, accepting a job offer or moving home. Think back to when you made the decision. Provide as much information as possible as to how the decision was made, who was involved and the criteria used to make the decision.

Finally, outline what has changed between then and now that makes you feel your decision, if made now, would be different. How do you act towards yourself for making that earlier decision?

Over time, our preferences, desires and understanding change, and yet so often we continue on a tried and tested path that has worked for us in the past. Be prepared to change your responses, your understanding and desires rather than resist them as immature and unreliable. Accept that we each live in a subjective world which constantly changes as our life unfolds. Enjoy the uniqueness of this experience and don't search for the 'one objective way' of doing things. It doesn't exist. It is a Myth. What does exist is your ability to access what is right for you.

What have your answers told you about yourself? The reasons for the initial decision might have seemed valid at the time, but in light of new information, the action you took may now seem outdated, unwise or even ridiculous. You might berate yourself or ask, 'How could I possibly have done this? Why was I so stupid as not to see the consequences of my actions?' There is little point in beating yourself up over something that has passed and which, at the time, was done for perfectly valid reasons. Learn to honour the decisions you make. Appreciate that you can only act with the knowledge and understanding you have at the time. Real freedom comes from the awareness and belief that the decisions you make can be changed in light of new information and knowledge. However, if you act as if decisions are set in stone and irreversible, you will automatically look to others to validate your decisions. Who wouldn't, when so much could be at stake? Be prepared to change what you believe to be true in the light of new information.

I do not deny that it is scary to act in a way which is sometimes contrary to the expectations of others, particularly those close to us. It takes commitment, and as Rollo May says:

> *Commitment is the healthiest when it is not without doubt, but in spite of doubt. To believe fully and at the same time to have doubts is not at all a contradiction: it presupposes a greater respect for truth, an awareness that truth always goes beyond anything that can be said or done at any given moment.*[4]

There will never be enough information to make the correct decision – the correct decision does not exist. What does exist is the knowledge that you are making decisions which you have chosen from your own subjective standpoint and which you may change in light of new information.

Each of us acts in order to bring about the consequences we desire. Ask yourself, 'What do I really want in my life?' Your answer may be a long-term partner, money, a house by the sea, a community of like-minded people. As things in themselves these are meaningless. What they do for us is to raise certain psychological and emotional states that we desire. We may desire money because it will give us the freedom to explore, a house because we believe it will offer us security, or a close-knit community because we want to belong. Beware of wanting something because others at your 'apparent' stage of life have it! The promise of it bringing you happiness is often a Myth.

Take a step back from the apparent benefits of having what you want. Instead, ask yourself, 'What is the situation I want to achieve by having these things?' In general, people do things to achieve a feeling of happiness or to avoid unhappiness. However we often engage in activities that appear to bring us more pain. This only points to our uniqueness – we engage in things that we desire or which we are used to. The man who constantly returns to a bullying partner may do so because it is a situation he desires, simply because it is consistent with his image of himself and his worth. It is not until he changes that internal image and accepts that he is free to choose, that he will seek out more meaningful situations rather than engaging in behaviour that has become reinforced over time. He may choose to continue with bullying partners – but this time he will question his choice from a position of strength. I imagine, though, that with greater insight, he might choose to change this pattern.

Let us return to the question, 'What do I really want in my life?' In answering this question, it is my experience that people find it much easier to say what they don't want. When asked what they do want, they flounder and talk in general terms about happiness, respect, freedom and security. However they often don't know what to do to achieve these states; they only know what they don't want to do because presumably this brings about the opposite state of affairs. They also look to other people to find the answers. Try this exercise for yourself.

Your answers to these questions will provide you with valuable insight into how much freedom you currently exercise in your life. If you find you are able to answer the first question more easily, it indicates that your motivation stems from trying to avoid unpleasant states. If you can more easily access what you want, then you are more motivated by producing desirable states more positively and directly. The source of your motivation will also influence your mood – it is your choice whether you stave off unhappiness or whether you actively seek a sense of well-being and mastery over your life.

The language we use often indicates whether we are acting positively towards achieving something or negatively away from something. Aim for the positive orientation. For instance, 'What sort of environmental activism would really provide me with a sense of fulfilment?' rather than, 'By joining a climate-change march, I will feel less guilty than not doing anything at all.' Aim to do things that bring about desirable states of mind rather than ways of minimising unhappiness.

Exercise 7

What don't you want in your life? Outline the things you don't want to do or the situations you don't want to find yourself in. What would it be like to find yourself with those things in your life? How would you describe your resultant state of mind?

Now ask yourself, 'What do I want in my life? What would I really like to do with my time and what experiences would I like to be having?' How would you describe your state of mind when you have the things you so desire?

The more you accept your freedom and exercise your choices meaningfully, the more you will be able to act positively towards getting what you want.

Exercise 8

Outline the things you currently do that bring you pleasure and happiness. This may be spending time with your partner, reading a novel, or having a swim. What percentage of your time is spent doing things you truly want to do?

Now outline the things you currently do to avoid discomfort or unhappiness. What percentage of your time is spent doing things out of duty or a sense of obligation?

It can be a salient lesson to consider the amount of time you spend doing things you truly enjoy rather than those done to avoid further pain. The problem with making negative decisions, i.e. those which avoid things becoming worse, is that we settle for less than we are capable of or are able to achieve. Then the Identity Myth tells us that this is all there is. The unhappy relationship, the unfulfilling job, or ungrateful in-laws are tolerated in an endeavour to minimise the possibility of more upset or conflict. Time and energy are wasted in staving off unhappiness, which is self-defeating behaviour because it is based on the belief in scarcity that 'this is as good as it gets.'

I remember two women talking to each other whilst queuing to have a swim. On reaching the pool, the friends learnt that it was closed because of a faulty temperature gauge. Instead of disappointment, one woman said, 'Fantastic – now I can go home and yet not feel guilty that I haven't done any exercise today!' This is a wonderful example of being motivated by negative decisions. The implication of the woman's comment was that she didn't really want to swim but that guilt or self-criticism was motivating her. If this were so, who was the judge who would criticise her for not exercising?

She is the only one. The internal dialogue that berates her has probably been given a voice based on 'shoulds' and 'oughts' about exercise, rather than a real desire to enjoy a swim.

Determine what is right or wrong for you. Don't let social pressures define what is desirable or not in your life. You are free if only you can accept this fact. The Identity Myth decrees that you must do what is expected, that you must live up to a certain image and that you are odd or selfish if you don't. When you wear certain clothes, drive a certain car, or hold down a certain job purely to stay in line with others' expectations, you are allowing others to determine what you should be.

We make many attempts to break away from social expectations. However after a time, breaking away from what we believe society, family or others dictate may also become a safe option, because they represent an institutionalised form of turning against the norm. They then become a norm in themselves. The gap year or overseas experience from university where young people travel between study and work is now often accompanied with the claim: 'Enjoy the freedom while you can; when you have a sensible job this will not be possible.' It therefore becomes a form of revolt within very limited boundaries. A similar cry is heard when people marry, and others say, 'Enjoy your free time while you can; when children come along, you will not be able to.' Few people question whether or not they want to conform to having a 'sensible' job or children, although increasingly, numbers of people do so as they engage with their freedom.

The issue about freedom is not that you don't spend your time engaging in demanding work, nor that you don't have children. These activities can be rewarding for many. The issue is that you fully embrace freedom, consider your choices and make decisions with passion because they are going to bring about a state of well-being that you desire. Freedom means that you don't do things because they are expected or because everyone does them, so you would feel the odd one out if you didn't. Even the drop-out or traveller who appears to have embraced freedom from the rat race may be colluding with another social pressure from that group called Traveller.

When you allow others to convince you that you don't have the right to be different or challenge the status quo, you are denying your own identity and colluding with the Identity Myth.

I recall a young man who, after studying languages at university, spent two long summers as a tour guide in the Mediterranean. He loved the opportunity to use his languages whilst exploring different countries. However, after the second term as a tour guide, family and peer pressures caused him to doubt the rightness of his decision. He felt that perhaps their claims that he should think of his future and begin a career in international banking were right. He gave up guiding and joined a large merchant bank in the UK, but still harks back to those enjoyable days as a tour guide. I remember thinking how sad it was that he could not honour his desire to do something he loved in exchange for the promise of security in the future.

The pressure that comes from others to conform, although offered in apparent good faith, is really an act of selfishness. By bowing to the norm against our wishes, we inadvertently reinforce the decisions others have made. To break free and act against the norm to conform not only honours our own freedom but often benefits others. For example, our non-conformity might cause others to question the reasons for their own decisions. However, this may not be something they wish to do.

Change

Contemporary films like *American Beauty* or *Duets* encourage us to reflect on society's expectations of what is desirable and the costs and benefits of slavishly adhering to goals set down by others. Who was it that said, 'You should have a career; you must have children; you must have a top-of-the-range car?' Decide what is right for you and then act in such a way to bring it about. Get in touch with your uniqueness and identity. Don't identify with another person, label or expectation of what others think you should be. By all means consider what others do, learn from their exercising their own choices, but do so in order to reinforce the fact that you are free to choose your own way of being.

In the same way that we develop our identity in line with others, we often assume that the identities of other people are similar. This causes us to expect them to do things and provide things that they can't. For example, it is the Identity Myth that says that parents must provide money for their adult children and that they should make their decisions to incorporate the needs of their children throughout their entire lives. These expectations arise in many spheres of life. You meet someone whose company you really enjoy but end up saying, 'They are wonderful but if only they would do ...' Very soon you focus on how you can change the person. This desire to change is incorporated in words such as 'I know he is capable of achieving more than he has, so I am going to convince him to start up his own business.' This may be interpreted as support and seeing an opportunity the other person can't see. However, more often it is because you want to change the person to bring about a state you desire. Not only are you denying them their freedom; you are giving away your power when you invest your energy in changing another to bring about your own dreams.

This also happens at a social level. A woman may attempt to stop her partner telling people something about her personal life because it is embarrassing. Embarrassing for whom? Are we mere appendages of others so that our own image of self is embarrassed by the actions of another? Surely the person sharing the information, telling the joke or dancing on the table only has himself or herself to answer to. By relinquishing our freedom, we give our power to others and are unduly influenced by their actions. It is the same as saying, 'That person insulted/humiliated me.' No one can insult or humiliate you without your permission. What our parents, our partner, or our friends do does not have to reflect on us at all. We come to believe it does because we choose to believe it. If we acknowledge our freedom and develop our own identity, then we are truly responsible only for our own behaviour. Of course, if we have children, we are responsible for their care and upbringing. But it is a Myth that we have to relinquish our identity and choices within the parenting role. We can choose to spend time with others, but do not expend your energy trying to change them. Instead, enjoy another's uniqueness and acknowledge and appreciate their own distinct personality with its own expression. Look for people who bring out the best in you rather than trying to change others.

Breaking Your Own and Others' Identity Myth

The Identity Myth implies that:

- You should be someone other than the person you want to be
- Fitting in with others' expectations and desires will bring you happiness

How can you avoid the Identity Myth ruling your life and point it out in others?

- Don't allow others to dictate the direction or operation of your life.
- Value your uniqueness and get in touch with your own needs, desires and expectations.
- Don't do things out of duty or obligation to others. Instead, challenge your life choices and question the amount of real commitment and choice they contain.
- Respect others' identity and uniqueness. Accept and learn from those differences, and enjoy the similarities.
- Do not use social norms and stereotypical expectations to judge your own and others' intentions.
- Do not try to change other people's behaviour. Instead, focus on changing your reactions to them and choose the type of people you want in your life.
- Be prepared to change your values and outlook as your life unfolds. Enjoy the uniqueness of the experience and don't search for an objective 'right' or 'wrong' - life is subjective.
- Be prepared to feel some anxiety when you act in ways contrary to the expectations of others. Accept that nothing works without commitment and that it is healthiest not when it is without doubt but in spite of it.
- People act to bring about physical and emotional well-being. Try to act in a positive way to bring about things you desire rather than avoid things you do not.

Chapter 3

The Selfishness Myth

You are selfish if you put your own needs before those of others.

Selfishness and Living Authentically

Sartre's notion of existential freedom suggests we must take responsibility for who we are, or fall prey to the myth that we have no choice. It suggests that there is no objective view of right or wrong and the individual must take full responsibility for all his or her actions or choices since there is no human nature and no objective rightness for those choices.

Many of the choices we make have implications for others which may be unpleasant or distressing. Decisions made in the name of 'being true to oneself' imply selfishness. However, to not act in conjunction with one's own conscience is deemed inauthentic. Could it be that we can live authentically and that what could be deemed our selfish actions are really an opportunity for others to learn from our example?

Sartre's views have been criticised as painting a picture of the human condition as selfish, particularly in view of there being no external rightness for our choices. However, he says that our choices always have implications for others since, 'I am thus responsible for myself and for all men, as I am creating a certain image of man as I would have him to be.'[5]

Throughout history, there appears to have been a popular ideal that it is valuable, righteous and even desirable to put your own needs and happiness second. People who apparently put the needs of others before their own are often seen as good, honest and 'better' people; the world would simply be a better place if only people could be more unselfish. Religious doctrine, in particular, has perpetuated these values, encouraging people to be 'dead to self' and think of others before themselves. It appears that this is done with the purpose of creating a better world comprised of unselfish people putting the needs and desires of others before their own.

I am unsure as to why this value is still so prevalent, despite apparent selfishness and mirroring of those who indulge in meeting their goals at all costs. Why is it that being selfish is considered undesirable? Why is it that acting in ways to bring about your own happiness is considered to be wrong?

In the last chapter, we saw that people act in ways that will bring about happiness or avoid discomfort. People live in all sorts of ways with the underlying belief that it will make them happy, even if they see others who are apparently unhappy doing the same thing. Little thought is given to the fact that others have very different needs and subjective views of the world. It is my own belief that the world would be a better place if people could be more selfish. What do I mean by this statement?

First, we have to define what being selfish actually is. One of the meanings of 'selfish' is 'of the self.' How can we not be ourselves? It is not possible for us to experience being in the world as not a self. We would not be alive if we were not experiencing some sense of continuity of our self, which is constantly enhanced and created through interactions with others. We are in a process of 'becoming' through relationships with others. Consider the following exercise to get in touch with this process.

Exercise 9

a) Think of a person in your life with whom you feel really good. When you are with them they appear to bring out the very best in you. Write down the ways in which you behave when you are with them. What and how do you discuss things? What are your mannerisms and facial expressions? What adjectives would you use to explain how you feel? Write down as much about your interactions with them as possible.

b) Now think of a person with whom you feel uncomfortable. When you are with them you appear to be anxious, subdued or irritated. It is as if they bring out the very worst in you. Write down as much about your interactions with them as possible.

In considering these questions, it is clear that other people have a profound influence on who we are and how we behave. This may seem obvious, but the reasons for our responses are often a little misguided. Popular beliefs are that some people 'bring out the best' in us and others 'the worst.' If we go along with this interpretation, we are reducing ourselves to mere objects which comprise a myriad of attributes and qualities. These different qualities emerge when others come into our presence. When they go away, those qualities are no longer brought to the fore but go back into the box for later. This is the basis of modern personality theory: that we comprise of a set of attributes and predispositions in varying proportion relative to others. We tend to see ourselves and others as having a certain temperament. I tend to be outgoing and optimistic whilst another is seen as morose and pessimistic. In this way, the character is seen as a fixed entity, as if inside each individual there is a pre-ordained mechanism.

There does, however, seem to be a consistency to our lives. How can we explain this consistency of character and experience which does not label each person and attribute their actions to some inner principle which they can never alter? One way is to use R. D. Laing's concept of the Existential Position. Laing defined this as 'the person's experience of his world and of himself.' As a psychotherapist, Laing saw his role as seeking to understand another's existential position. In other words, obtaining some understanding of the individual's unique, inner experience of 'their' world. Laing offers as an example one of his patients who said he was made of glass and was terrified of being shattered. This may sound unusual, but a closer look at the language people commonly use provides clear evidence for very different existential positions. The role of therapy, to a large extent, is to work with an individual to challenge the value and usefulness of existing existential positions.

Each of us holds a fixed attitude at any given time and often over quite long periods of time. The language people use indicates what this position may be. Phrases like 'to be honest' or, 'quite frankly' are telling. Before we consider interpreting these, think about the phrases that you regularly use.

Common phrases would include:

- To be honest
- Quite frankly
- I can't blame you
- In an ideal world
- I can't help being a bit concerned
- It's only to be expected, but...
- In this day and age
- In the good old days

Exercise 10

Think of phrases that you regularly use that might indicate your existential position, e.g. 'to be honest' or 'quite frankly.' You may be aware of these, want to change them, or are told by others that your remarks indicate scepticism or anticipated antagonism. Write down your phrases and next to them an explanation of the value to you of using them.

'To be honest' might indicate that the person is about to say something that is unacceptable or contentious.

'Quite frankly' indicates a person whose existential position is that of being distrusted.

'I can't blame you' might come from someone whose perspective is one of constant betrayal and disappointment.

'In an ideal world' reveals a person whose existential position is a feeling of the unyielding hardness of the world.

'I can't help being a bit concerned' comes from a person who feels overwhelmed by a myriad of concerns.

'It's only to be expected' suggests a feeling of anticipated failure and disappointment.

'In this day and age' suggests a belief in a much wider and encompassing source of information that is appropriate because of its ubiquity.

'In the good old days' suggests a feeling of disappointment with the present and a desire to resort to happier times.

Another way is to see ourselves not as fixed objects but as beings who are created through interactions with others. Thus someone who is seen as having the quality of 'sociability' probably doesn't have this quality all boxed up somewhere in their personality.

Instead, it is through relationship with another that this quality is created. The person experiences themselves as sociable because it is created through the interaction, not because it purely 'comes out of the box' as sociability.

This is not to say that people are not predisposed to behave in certain ways, but maybe there is a different way of looking at these predispositions which allows more flexibility and change. Indeed, if we weren't predisposed to behave in certain ways, there would be no sense of permanence and uniqueness when alone. It is saying that we are not fixed entities but are created through our interactions with others. People do not 'bring out the best' or 'worst' in us. Therefore, our sense of self is created through being with others.

Let's go back to the selfishness argument. I stated that the world would be a better place if each of us were more selfish. I believe that if people were to put more time, attention and care into being who they truly want to be and to be the best they can be, then they would benefit others. This would occur for a number of reasons:

- They would be honest in their interaction with others and say what they want and what they mean.
- They would not be resentful of the sacrifices they inevitably end up making by trying to be unselfish.
- They would be good examples to others of 'putting their own house in order' instead of trying to impose their values on others.
- They would be focusing on changing themselves and their reactions to others rather than trying to change others.

The fact is that we are all selfish because we are trying to do things that we believe will make us happy. However, there are still the cries that it is selfish not to put others before yourself, which causes guilt in many who try to resist this. But what would happen if everyone gave up their happiness to make someone else happy?

Example

Think of the ability to be happy and fulfilled as a brightly decorated present. Everyone has one of these presents but they don't open it. In order to be unselfish, each person has to pass their present on to another person because they have to put another's happiness first. The only problem is that the receiving person is selfish if they open it, so they pass it on to another person. The result is that no one has the ability to be happy and fulfilled.

What is the point therefore of being unselfish? Would it be a better world? Who would you be unselfish for? Who would benefit from constantly considering the happiness of others and denying their own fulfilment? Ultimately, there would have to be a selfish person somewhere to receive the gift in order for someone else to be happy.

If we take the perspective that we are created through our interactions, you could argue that you are more selfish by not considering your own happiness first, since your unhappy interactions with others will influence them and create their sense of self. The greatest way, therefore, to contribute to others is to make yourself happy and then their interactions with you will be more rewarding.

The Selfishness Myth invariably influences parents who allegedly make extreme sacrifices for the future happiness of their children. They may stay in undesirable jobs which take too much of their time, they pay excessive mortgages so their children can live in large homes, they provide a taxi service for their children to the extent that they have no time left for themselves. All this is done in the name of being unselfish for their children. They then ultimately avoid realising any of the capital in their homes in order to be able to leave it to their children after their death. And what happens when the children, as adults, acquire this wealth? They do the same for their own children. It is no different than passing on that present labelled 'ability to be happy.' Each person, in an endeavour to be unselfish, relinquishes living their life NOW for some belief in the future happiness of another. The cycle continues and no one is living the life they want to live.

I am not saying that we do not have responsibilities for the care of children. Quite clearly, the choice to have children involves providing a level of support and care for them. What I am saying is that to totally deny your own needs in order to be unselfish is a fruitless pursuit, which ultimately results in no one being happy.

Exercise 11

Think of a time in your life when someone labelled your actions as selfish. Write down the reasons they gave you for labelling you as such. What was your response to their criticisms and what were your reactions? What did you do as a result of their negative evaluation of you?

Many people find it very difficult to maintain their choices in the face of criticism and claims that they are selfish. Depending on what caused another to label you as selfish will, to a large extent, determine your response. Being labelled as selfish for keeping someone waiting at the cinema for two hours is probably not as difficult to cope with as leaving a marriage to pursue your own happiness. The reasons people give for saying you are selfish are often accompanied by elements of the Identity Myth. Typical reasons include:

- You are a selfish mother – good mothers should not go out to work when the children are young.
- If you were a good partner you would visit my parents as they grow old.
- What sort of father are you, spending all weekend playing football when you should be with your family?

Whenever you hear the words 'should,' 'must' or 'ought,' the Selfishness Myth is underpinning the values of the speaker. Often people labelled as selfish moderate their behaviour because they are negatively motivated by the anxiety caused by such criticism. However, the accusers are in fact being selfish themselves. They may even criticise someone in an endeavour to change them for their own ends, feel less selfish themselves, or justify why they conform to the social norm of 'selflessness.'

People often criticise others for things they don't actually like about themselves. It is easier to project the criticism onto another person than change something in themselves. However, the person pursuing happiness by trying to change another, or by changing to avoid discomfort is in a very precarious position. They are giving the responsibility for their happiness to others and that is a very risky place to be.

Advocating selfishness doesn't mean that you don't do things for others to show appreciation, affection or to make them feel good. I am saying that it is a Myth that it will bring about happiness if you do things to avoid being called selfish. People often claim that they are happy when doing things for others, and that may be true. However, in the process they are selfishly deriving benefits from their actions – and this is okay!

Remember that all acts are ultimately selfish – of the self – and performed to bring about a sense of well-being. Even Mother Theresa, with all her hard work and effort which brought about relief and support for many, was operating from a position of selfishness. By devoting her life to others, she brought about a sense of happiness and fulfilment that was greater than what could have been derived from pursuing another avenue. And her selfishness resulted in a lot of happiness for other people. Nelson Mandela, a man believed to epitomise unselfishness, wisely suggested that by being the best we can be, we offer more to others. Quoting Marianne Williamson in his inaugural address as President of South Africa in 1994, he said:

> *Our deepest fear is not that we are inadequate. Our deepest fear is that we are powerful beyond measure. It is our light, not our darkness that most frightens us. We ask ourselves, 'Who am I to be brilliant, gorgeous, talented, fabulous?' Actually, who are you not to be? You are a child of God. Your playing small doesn't serve the world. There's nothing enlightened about shrinking so that other people won't feel insecure around you. We are meant to shine, as children do. And as we let our own light shine, we unconsciously give other people permission to do the same. As we're liberated from our own fear, our presence automatically liberates others.*

Nevertheless, be prepared to experience some anxiety in seeking to pursue your own happiness and freedom. Parents who do not slavishly give their lives for their children's happiness are often pilloried as self-centred and unfit parents. Partners who leave their spouses are criticised for causing the other person so much pain. Children who do not pursue the career decreed by their parents, who gave them the best schooling, are seen as ungrateful. Maybe the people casting these criticisms are themselves selfish, wanting others to be like them in order to justify their own life choices. So often people are negatively motivated to avoid feeling unselfish. However, in doing this they are choosing from a few alternatives for happiness. A real sense of freedom will only come about when they are positively motivated to bring about the sense of well-being that they desire, not trying to avoid the feeling they dislike. The Selfishness Myth operates when people's behaviour is dictated by 'shoulds,' 'oughts,' or 'musts.'

Exercise 12

What could you say to someone who calls you selfish? What can you do to maintain your choices and yet live with the anxiety of being labelled selfish or even being ostracised by others who criticise you? Write down your answers to these questions, using the example you provided in Exercise 11.

There are many ways you can respond to the criticism of being selfish. Each of them involves a level of assertiveness and conviction that your choices are right for you. However, it does not involve being aggressive, since a level of defensiveness will result in others questioning your own conviction in your claims. I believe it is always useful to acknowledge what is being said to you directly and then respond in an assertive and direct way.

Let us consider each of the following examples of reasons for being selfish and consider suitable responses

Example 1

Criticism: You are a selfish mother – good mothers should not go out to work when their children are young.

Response: I appreciate that you believe mothers of young children should not work. I equally have beliefs regarding the care and support of children. However, this does not include not working outside of the home when I can properly provide for their care for the short time I am not with them. I make every effort to ensure that they are safe and happy in my absence and that they benefit from the work I do outside the home.

The response to the last example of course depends on who is doing the criticising. In the criticism, it is assumed that the person doing the criticising is directly involved in the parenting/childcare. If it were someone else, perhaps a more suitable response would relate to assertively stressing that the matter had little to do with people outside of the family unless they were in some way responsible for the welfare of the children.

Example 2

Criticism: If you were a good partner you would visit my parents as they grow old.

Response: I appreciate that you believe your aged parents should be cared for. However, I do not believe it follows that, as your husband, it is my duty to visit them to provide this care. I believe there are two separate issues here – the first is expectations regarding me as your husband and the second, the care of aged parents. Can we separate these two issues and not link the care of your parents with some sense of duty and obligation on my part because I am your husband?

Example 3

Criticism: What sort of father are you spending all weekend playing football when you should be with your family?

Response: It appears that you believe that to be good parents fathers should spend all weekend with their families. I appreciate that this is your belief but I do enjoy football and sometimes this occurs at the weekends. Let's sit down and discuss how we can divide our time so that we, as parents, spend time with our children but also have time to do the things we enjoy on our own.

It is often relatively easy to learn new assertiveness techniques to deal with the criticisms of others regarding our behaviour. However, this does not necessarily mean we are really exercising the choices that are available to us. Longer-lasting change in attitudes may take longer. Choosing the life we want to live begins with deep personal change of our values and a belief that we are ultimately free and may choose to live our life in whatever way we choose.

Compromise versus Exchange?

It is often assumed that we must sacrifice our wishes for the benefit of others and that others should make sacrifices for us. This is clearly seen in the values many people hold around personal relationships. People talk in terms of compromise and 'giving up' selfish desires to fit in with another. What about seeing relationships in terms of sources of exchange? When we choose to do something in life, presumably we prefer to do or have this one thing in preference to something else. For example, when we buy a car, we prefer the option of independent travel to that of money in the bank.

We benefit from owning a car and the vendor benefits from the money received in the exchange.

Life is made up of millions of exchanges where each partner in the exchange receives something they value more than what they give up. This may be measured in terms of time, effort, or money. Mutually beneficial relationships operate when the desires of both parties are compatible. This happens in every aspect of our life. Some desires may be the same – two people decide to go out to dinner together. Others are different – I enjoy good food and you enjoy cooking. When desires are compatible, there is no need for either party to make sacrifices. The Selfishness Myth operates when people compromise and make sacrifices where their desires are not compatible.

I remember a personal experience of going to the cinema with a new friend. We didn't know each other very well and each had little idea of the type of movie the other would enjoy. After much deliberation, we chose a film and later found that we had both sat through a movie that was totally unrewarding and unlike the films each of us normally saw. This was a good example of compromise and sacrifice. Each of us, in an endeavour not to appear selfish, had held back our real views on the attractiveness of the film and, as a result, saw a film that was disagreeable to both of us. No one was happy through us each trying to appear unselfish.

The selfish person is aware of the needs and desires of others and sees them as opportunities to enter into mutually beneficial exchanges. They don't sacrifice themselves for others or expect others to do the same. Instead of trying to change other people's behaviour by labelling them as selfish, look for people with whom you know you can develop mutually beneficial relationships so that sacrifice is not necessary.

People find happiness in different ways and whilst it may appear they do this by being unselfish, this is not the case. Recognise also that when someone says you are being selfish, they are actually being selfish themselves. They are upset that you are not doing what they selfishly want you to do.

Breaking Your Own and Others' Selfishness Myth

The Selfishness Myth is that you are selfish if you put your needs before those of others. In reality, being selfish entails taking responsibility for the direction of your life and examining the options for your happiness.

How can you avoid the Selfishness Myth ruling your life and point it out in others?

- Get in touch with your own needs and desires and seek ways to satisfy them.
- Recognise that the word 'selfish' means 'of the self' and you cannot experience the world as fully as you might without full commitment to yourself and your dreams.
- Who we are is created through interactions with others, so surround yourself with people who are good for you and offer you the greatest opportunity to meet your own needs.
- Become more selfish in order to increase the honesty and communication with the people in your life.
- Don't sacrifice your own happiness for that of others. Such behaviour is self-defeating for yourself and others who perpetuate this Myth.
- Recognise that when people call you selfish they are upset that you are not doing what they selfishly want you to do.

- Develop assertive ways in which you can positively respond to others' claims that you are selfish. Focus on changing your beliefs about the 'rightness' of acting in ways to bring about your own happiness.
- Recognise that by becoming more selfish you offer others the best example of how we can each take responsibility for our own happiness.

Chapter 4

The Group Myth

It is better to be part of a group than to be an individual.

Dasein as a Potentiality

Numerous existential writers remind us of the difficulty we find in accepting our freedom to choose how we want to be. Instead we look to others to define what is appropriate and to dictate the direction of our lives. Sartre talks of us adopting the cover of Bad Faith, whereby we fool ourselves that we do not have choice but adopt ways of being that mirror what we see others doing around us. Nietzsche talks of the Herd, and Heidegger of the They-Self, both of which suggest the influence of others on our own choices of how to be.

Heidegger says we can either collude with the demands of the They-Self (the world of others and our perception of their expectations and social conventions), or heed what he calls the Call of Conscience and become aware of our choice of how to be against the backcloth of our temporal existence.

In order to understand Heidegger, the concept of Dasein must be grasped as a new way of understanding the meaning of Being. Dasein means 'being there' and for Heidegger this always means in relationship and never in isolation. For instance, Mitsein means 'Being-in-the-world-with-others.'

For Heidegger, the world cannot be what he calls, 'bracketed' ie. simplified or separated from anything else.: 'The world is always the one I share with others. The world of Dasein is a with-world.'[6] This contradicts Cartesian dualistic ideas and contemporary scientific methods of deconstructing aspects of individual experience for analysis and observation. Dasein is not an actual thing, but the possibility of various ways of being.

He says we have not chosen the world into which we are thrown: our family, culture, gender, position in history and unique circumstances. This constitutes our 'thrown-ness' and after being thrown, we have choices over 'how' we want to be. By responding to a way of being portrayed by 'they' or Das Man, we are living inauthentically, in that we do not consider the possibility of other ways of being or the various options for responding to life's challenges.

Thus we can collude with our perception of others' expectations or engage with our own freedom and live authentically. Authenticity is not about genuineness or being real, nor is inauthenticity about being false. Instead, 'Authenticity is the moment when Dasein confronts Being as it is, "ready for anxiety"[7] as it is anxiety that Dasein tried to avoid in its "dispersal" into the generality of the they.'[8]

For the majority of us, the family is the first group into which we are born/thrown. It offers us the opportunity to learn, develop, grow and be socialised into wider society. For many of us, the family provides a source of identity and security within which we can flourish and grow as individuals. For others, the family is a source of control and limitation with expectations being imposed which have little connection with who or how we want to be. Long after we have left the family into which we are born, the ideals, values, and expectations we learnt within the family follow us. From our earliest experiences, the Group Myth impinges on our life to the extent that we can lose a real sense of who we and others are. Cooper, albeit critically, sums this up by saying:

> *One of the first lessons one is taught in the course of one's family conditioning is that one is not enough to exist in the world on one's own. One is instructed in great detail to disown one's self and to live agglutinatively so that one glues bits of other people onto oneself and then proceeds to ignore the difference between the otherness in one's self and the self-sameness of one's self. This is alienation in the sense of a passive submission to invasion by others, originally the family others.*[9]

Such conditioning continues throughout our lives. It is often believed that you can accomplish more by sharing responsibilities, efforts and rewards than by acting alone. In many situations, this might be true, particularly if the individuals in the encounter meaningfully choose to share their efforts. However, in many cases, our efforts might stem from a fear of being alone, or lack of self-confidence in the rightness of our own goals. Thus, the rewards of shared endeavours are promised to result out of our personal relationships, social encounters, and organisations. Common catchphrases reinforce this belief:

- There is safety in numbers
- In union there is strength
- The whole is greater than the sum of its parts

In organisations, for example, large sums of time, money and effort are spent on trying to maximise team effort to enhance individual, group and organisational performance. Large sums of money are spent on team-building and training, despite an awareness and active encouragement of individual competition for limited rewards.

Exercise 13

Think of a group you belong to or have belonged to in the past. This may be a work group or a social group. Write down the objective of that group and the benefits that you consider you receive(d) from being a member. Then write down the disadvantages that you experience(d) or which you heard others complain of.

Let us consider work groups here because this is often the means through which people experience regular and sustained group interactions. Similar situations also operate in social or family groups, often with different language to describe the dynamics.

Back in the 1930s in America, Elton Mayo's pioneering research highlighted the social nature of work behaviour. This subsequently influenced management training to incorporate social and psychological reward systems as well as financial ones. Management effort and systems now take this into account and continually seek ways to facilitate effective group working. Benefits are believed to exist for all those involved in group effort:

- Pooling of ideas and generation of new ones
- Motivation of members to contribute
- Creativity and synergy derived from group interaction
- Sharing of knowledge
- Specialisation of effort
- Improvement in morale
- Maximisation of individuals' preferred team behaviour/style.

However, a number of negative outcomes seem to accompany or even cancel out these benefits. Let us consider some of them, namely:

- Conformity to group norms
- 'Groupthink' (explained below)
- Diluting effective decision-making
- Typecasting of individual personality types, disallowing other behaviours.

Conformity to Group Norms

If an individual is a member of a group which they value and wish to be part of, they will find that, at times, they will have to moderate their behaviour if they are to be accepted. Norms – collective, allegedly shared, agreed ways of behaving in a group – are major determinants of members' behaviour. Individuals who act in ways counter to these norms become subject to enormous pressure to moderate their behaviour. These pressures may be direct and imply expulsion from the group if they don't conform. They may be covert and involve alienation, non-involvement in or access to group activities and exchange of information. The individual has a choice – they can stay and conform or leave because the pressure to conform becomes too powerful.

However, this involves compromise and as soon as you compromise, you are minimising your chances of achieving your own unique objectives, desires and expectations. Ironically, this may be the case for the majority of the members in a group. Let me give you an example.

I remember conducting an attitude survey in a large public relations company in the UK. The answers to two of the questions struck me as very important indicators of the strength of organisational culture and norms. The two questions and response options read:

1. On average, how many hours of overtime do you work every day?

- None at all
- Less than one hour
- 1–2 hours
- 2–3 hours
- 3 hours plus

2. If you work overtime on a regular basis, how concerned are you with this arrangement?

1 2 3 4 5 6

Very concerned ←→ Not concerned at all

Over 70% of employees replied that they worked in excess of three hours overtime per day. Of this 70%, 85% circled response number 1, indicating they were very concerned with the amount of overtime they worked. Subsequent open-ended questions indicated serious unhappiness, resentment and even anger at the pressure – spoken and unspoken – put upon them by the organisation to do this. Thus, the vast majority of employees were behaving in ways that made them seriously unhappy, presumably in the belief that they had no choice or that this compromise would ultimately contribute to them achieving their own personal objectives. Furthermore, they were blaming the organisation for their predicament when, in fact, they chose not to take responsibility for their actions and change their behaviour. Whatever their reasons and justifications for their behaviour, the fact remains that those employees were spending large amounts of their life *now* doing something that made them unhappy.

Exercise 14

Can you think of an example where your behaviour at work or in a social group appeared to be influenced by the prevailing group norms? What did this involve and where do you consider the pressure was coming from? What was the cost of conforming to those influences to change your preferred behaviour?

Where is this pressure coming from? I don't deny that managers can act on real and implied threats where people don't conform. Ultimately, you could be passed over for promotion, demoted, given a poor reference, fired, or suffer intolerable discomfort and anxiety. But, as in the case above, the majority of the employees were themselves perpetuating a culture that reinforced the belief that 'management' were somehow imposing this pressure and the belief of 'that's just the way things are done around here!' Culture and norms are constantly reinforced by the members who blame some collective belief system, when in fact the desires and beliefs of the contributing members may be counter to what is stated and acted upon.

Thus, adherence to group norms limits our freedom and ultimate means of realising our objectives. What we must realise is that if we stay in such an oppressive system, it is OUR CHOICE. We are choosing to feel exploited – in fact, we have given permission for this to happen. To blame the culture, norms or group pressures for our behaviour is ultimately a cop–out. We can choose to change the way we respond to these pressures.

> **Example**
>
> When I worked as a university lecturer, I recall one of my students taking a job at a large American investment bank in the UK. He was a trainee dealer and arrived at the bank at 7.30 am on his first day. At 8.00 pm that night he was tired and eager to go home. However, no one except the administrators had left despite the leaving time in everyone's contract being 5.30pm. Thus, he packed up his desk, got his coat and headed for the door. His movements were accompanied with a collective slow handclap from his colleagues who chorused, 'So you are going to be a part-timer eh?' The message here is all too apparent. He had violated the cultural norm that in order to show commitment and be successful in this company, one had to be seen to stay late, and out of choice. I wonder how many of those people secretly wished they had the confidence to leave too.
>
> Sadly, it was the last time the new recruit left before the others – presumably he believed that this compromise, in the long term, would contribute to a bigger reward. Somehow I doubt it – he had just given others permission to impose even more pressure on him and the ultimate costs to his health, well-being and self-esteem were crippling.

Groupthink

The concept of Groupthink[10] was suggested by Janis to explain a variant of social conformity. Janis observed a number of top-level US government decisions that resulted in disastrous outcomes. However, upon reflection, the decision-makers questioned how they could have made such decisions which subsequently appeared naive and ill-advised. He gives the example of President Kennedy's team decision to support the Cuban exiles in their overthrow of Fidel Castro. This invasion was intercepted and Castro's retaliation resulted in the Cuban Missile Crisis of 1962 which, at that time, posed the biggest threat to world peace.

Upon reflection, Kennedy admitted that the decision was naïve and would most certainly have resulted in massive retaliation from Cuba. Other members of the White House admitted that they too were concerned with the possibility of this threat. Why did these members not speak out at the time? Apparently, they did not wish to upset the camaraderie and sense of cohesion that existed between the members. To raise concerns in the face of so much apparent support from others for the action would only have served to reduce the cohesiveness of the group.

Janis observed this process in other top-level decision-making groups during the escalation of the Vietnam War and America's involvement in the First World War. It has now become a valuable concept in organisational behaviour, with managers attempting to encourage members to question their decision-making and justify their team choices. However, the concept of Groupthink highlights the political nature of groups and the relinquishing of individual responsibility in collective decision-making.

Exercise 15

Think of an example when you have gone along with a group's decision despite personal doubts in the efficacy of the decision. This may be in a work group or in a social or family situation. What was involved and what was your personal reason for not raising your concerns? What was the personal cost to you of conforming to the collective decision?

Numerous examples exist of individuals conforming to perceived group pressure to act in a certain way, despite strong feelings against the collective decision. Often a fear of feeling foolish, of self-doubt in one's ability and expertise, and of wanting to be seen to be a supportive team player stops us speaking out.

In organisations, the cost can be huge and so often is justified in some face-saving exercise. However, the personal cost of this can be enormous despite the temporary feeling of belonging to a group. Our health, self-esteem and belief in our own knowing can be abused to such an extent that we may cease to trust ourselves at all. To continually act in ways that encourage us to ignore our insights and intuitions, is to reduce our freedom and means of realising our individual dreams and goals.

Diluting Effective Decision-making

We have seen that the effectiveness of decision-making is enormously influenced by being in a group. Whilst there may be a pooling of ideas and synergising effect of group endeavours, one sure thing is that the effectiveness of decisions in terms of measurable outcomes and member satisfaction will be affected. Early research indicated that in groups, the effectiveness of decisions was not as good as the best individual, but better than the average. Thus, there appeared to be a watering-down of expertise but enhancement of weaker contributions.

What organisations decide to do with this information is up to the managers who choose to take responsibility for doing something about this. But what about you as an individual seeking to realise your own objectives? Do you want to have your contributions diluted by less able members or the feeling that you are not powerful enough to go it alone?

Groups are not living entities. Groups do not think. Only individuals do. But teams and groups are based upon the assumption that the group's needs are more important than that of the individual members. Remember, in the group context, each member of the alleged collective has a different perspective. In an organisation, what you experience as your career and means of achieving your objectives is reduced to that of a human resource for the organisation. You are giving away your power if you leave your life in the hands of others, who, through some collective endeavour, believe everyone will be happy. Your happiness and achievement of your goals is your responsibility and not that of others.

Typecasting of Individual Personality Types

A vast number of personality questionnaires exist which categorise people according to different types or traits. These are invariably linked to the hope of predicting future behaviour either in the workplace or other aspects of social interaction. Whilst these may be useful yardsticks, they can become limiting and cause us to believe that our behaviour is fixed and largely unchangeable.

In group situations, many such team-type questionnaires exist and seek to look at individual contributions and the best combination of individual types to achieve collective outcomes. Such instruments may highlight predispositions and preferences to behave in a certain way, but they do have their negative aspects. People become labelled as having certain qualities or of being a certain type. Any indication of the expected behaviour is immediately reinforced with cries of, 'Oh that's typical of his type.' People become typecast, and any deviance from the type is ignored or minimised as others seek only confirmation of their earlier impressions and judgements.

Thus, individuality is further stifled with people attributing their own and others' behaviour to that of their 'type.' However, we are far more complex than any measuring instrument could imply. If used wisely, instruments may act as useful yardsticks to consider typical predispositions, but in group situations they become all-powerful and function as explanations for all possible actions. This is where the Group Myth meets the Identity Myth – the belief that it is better to be in a group and act in set, expected ways than to be an individual and creatively seek out ways to realise your own dreams.

But no need for isolation ...

What has been said earlier may imply that in order to be free and exercise choices, you must spend your time alone and no longer be part of group endeavours. This is not true. Clearly, our interests do overlap, but we must realise that each person has their own agenda and things that will make them happy. For some, this might mirror some of the things others do. For others, their choices might appear bizarre and contrary to what the majority believe will bring happiness. The things we might choose are as unique as the individuals we are. Also, some of our choices directly involve other people, as we can derive great pleasure from caring for and supporting others. However, it is a myth that being in a group, i.e. adhering to allegedly common goals, will provide you with the best opportunity to realise your goals. This invariably results in compromise and time needed to negotiate this compromise. In a group, the efforts and rewards are shared between the members. The effort you expend and the rewards you gain in a group amount to far less than if you were acting alone.

If you are working alone to achieve your desires, you can put 100% effort into this endeavour and reap 100% of the rewards. If you work in a group of two, the efforts and rewards are immediately reduced by half. You put 50% of the effort in and rely on the other person to put 50% in too. However, you can only control your own effort. As much as you encourage or cajole the other person, they will only put in the amount of effort that they choose to. In a group, of course, this becomes diluted by even more people. Thus you need to evaluate the significance of your actions and the resultant rewards. The more control you have over your actions to achieve the desired outcomes, the more incentive there is for the effort you put in.

So don't give your power away to others to get what you desire. Focus on what you want and who you want to be and then seek out opportunities to enter into exchanges with others who can exchange what you want for something they desire. They will then be equally motivated to give you what you want, since it will result in them receiving what they are seeking.

We can benefit from sharing our lives with others whilst still focusing on satisfying our own objectives. This can be done directly or indirectly. When faced with a situation, you can decide whether your action will result in what you want or not. For example, imagine you have embarked upon a training program to develop your skills base. However, you find that the course does not offer the particular modules that you wish to study. You have two broad choices (although we could break them down into further choices). The first is to try and change the minds and actions of others to bring about what you want. In our example, you could lobby the trainers to provide additional modules). Alternatively, you can consider what the situation offers, decide it doesn't provide you with what you want and look for it elsewhere. (In our example, this would mean it is unlikely that the program will change but that other programs exist and need to be explored.)

Thus, you can act directly or indirectly. Direct action puts you in control of your own effort and thus your rewards. Indirect action involves trying to persuade others to change their actions, and is less likely to be successful. A realistic and independent individual recognises the identity and uniqueness of themselves and others they interact with. You cannot change the identities or desires of others.

Thus, it is more effective to decide what best direct alternatives are available to you in view of the individual identities. People will only change when it makes sense to them.

Most people think of indirect ways of getting what they want. This applies to personal relationships as well as work situations. They focus on trying to change others' ideas and actions. But it doesn't work. The best direct alternative is to recognise and respect the identities and needs of others and decide if you will invest your time with them or whether you would be better off going elsewhere.

The common belief is that you must compromise with others if you are ever to have meaningful relationships with them. Try instead to think in terms of Accommodation of Needs. Compromise implies that neither party is happy, as they relinquish important aspects of what they desire. Accommodation suggests that you have relationships with people whose efforts and desires are compatible with your own. If you spend time with people with whom you are compatible, no one has to compromise because each is meeting their own self-interests. Also, by honouring your own needs, you give other people permission to get in touch with theirs. There is then great opportunity for us to interact with the uniqueness and humanness of others rather than hold expectations derived merely from role relationships.

Group efforts neutralise individual incentives to act by creating shared responsibilities, efforts and rewards. By putting yourself at the centre of your life with full responsibility for it, your efforts will be directly proportional to your rewards. You will also become a good example to others who spend their lives compromising and often resenting others because of that.

Breaking Your Own and Others' Group Myth

The Group Myth is that it is better to be part of a group than be an individual. How can you avoid the Group Myth ruling your life and point it out in others?

- Engage in direct action to achieve your objectives rather than indirectly encouraging people to change in line with your desires.
- Avoid conforming to the expectations and desires of groups. Instead, seek out people with whom you have positive interactions and who do not pressurise you to change in order to meet their own objectives.
- Recognise that adherence to group norms limits your freedom.
- Take responsibility for your behaviour. If you feel exploited, it is because you are choosing to allow this to happen. You can choose to change the way you respond to group pressures.
- Trust your own judgement and act on it rather than looking to others for confirmation.
- Recognise that groups do not think or act. Only individuals do this. You alone are responsible for your happiness and means of achieving this state.
- Remain sceptical of instruments and measurements that typecast individuals and predict their behaviour. Categorising leads to typecasting and limited beliefs about the scope and range of what we are capable of.
- Evaluate the significance of your actions and appreciate that if you are responsible for 100% of your rewards, then you will be motivated 100% to expend effort in order to realise them.
- Seek out people with whom you can have mutually satisfying exchanges which serve to meet your individual self-interests.

Chapter 5

The Commitment Myth

It is impossible to change certain things in our lives once we have committed to them.

The Ontic and the Ontological

Existential writers make a distinction between the Ontological and the Ontic. Ontology is the study of Existence. The Ontological comprises the existential givens which we do not choose and which are aspects of being. The Ontic comprises our responses to those givens or how we are at a particular time, given our capacity to choose.

Human beings have a special kind of Being in that they exist and relate to their Being and the capacity to be concerned and attend to it. Cohn[11] says some existential givens, which we all experience, include:

- Being-in-the-World
- Being-with-Others
- Being-in-a-Body
- Mortality
- Thrown-ness
- Temporality
- Language

Our Ontic experience is what we make of our existence within these 'givens' and anxiety results as we learn of its subjective and impermanent nature.

> The freedom to create our Being and experience others doing the same leads to uncertainty and the experience of existential anxiety. The resultant choice is between authenticity and the anxiety that meaningful living brings, or inauthenticity and existential guilt.
>
> By heeding the Call of Conscience, we are reminded of our potentiality of Being. Cohn[12] says, '...this conscience is not concerned with reminding us of the rules of 'morality' which are ontic, but rather calls us to the realisation of what our existence is essentially about – our openness to Being.'

It is a commonly-held belief that it is impossible to be free from the responsibilities of past decisions, and that restrictions in your life make it impossible to change. This is not true. In western society, much emphasis is placed on progression and success through career development as a means of achieving what we want as individuals. I have chosen to concentrate on this choice, and many of the examples offered will focus on work-related choices. However, the arguments put forward will also relate to other restrictions and choices in your life.

The existential view is that freedom is not a choice — we are 'doomed' to be free, but the responsibility and anxiety arising out of this realisation causes us to resist it. Accordingly, people adopt a variety of strategies to avoid embracing their freedom and exercising their choices. Let us examine this further.

Exercise 16

Think of something in your life that you would like to change. It may be something big like your career, relationship, or sense of duty. Alternatively, it might be how you spend your weekends or holidays. Briefly outline what you would like to change and then write down the reasons you give yourself for not changing.

Whilst the situation you chose might include various things you want to change, often the reasons for changing are similar. These tend to fall into two categories:

a) **Other people or situations are the cause of me not changing.**
Consider the typical excuses people use:
- I have responsibilities.
- It is a duty to to attend family events, even if their carnist eating habits cause me alarm.
- I have worked so hard to achieve what I have – how could I possibly give it all up?
- It has taken me ten years to get proficient at this job – what a waste of an investment if I change it all now.
- I trained for this profession – what a waste if I change careers at this stage.

b) **Choosing to avoid the reality of freedom.**
Consider the typical actions people take. They may:
- Develop habits and rituals they consider intrinsic to life itself.
- Decide the cost of change is too great.
- Choose to continue on a path which is safe but which no longer challenges them.
- Believe that working for someone else is a safe and predictable reality.

- Take time out to enjoy 'freedom,' like holidays and leisure, but these are equally well-organised and influenced by expectations of a desirable self-image.
- Tell their children not to be naïve when they challenge your routine, responding that 'when you are older, you will understand.'

Thus, people either choose to blame others for their lack of freedom, or a wider system of values which presupposes the way we must all live at different life stages. People believe they should be sensible and live sensible lives; in doing so, they protect themselves from the danger of real life by hiding behind a constructed security. They know 'real freedom' causes anxiety and so they opt for duty. However, life often reminds us that we are 'doomed' to be free.

Exercise 17

Think of a time in your life when something outside of your control threatened the secure environment you had created for yourself. This may be the loss of a job or an illness. Write down what this involved and what you felt at the time. Try to put a label to the emotions and thoughts that you experienced as a result of this.

There are many times in life when our secure and structured lives experience a wake-up call. What we thought was predictable and calm suddenly is not. The death of a loved one, retrenchment, terminal illness or accident reminds us of the fragile nature of security. The attack on the Pentagon and World Trade Centre in 2001 sent a wave of fear and disbelief across the world as people's structured beliefs about security were threatened. To embrace the possibility of attack on areas of life we believe are impermeable to change is to embrace the reality of our finiteness and fragile hold on life. The panic and fear that resulted from such attacks is so intense because it forces us to engage with life and question the very meaning of our existence. We can either scramble to salvage our routines using the tried and tested resources we have always used, or realise our finiteness, engage with our choices and carve out the life we want to live *now*.

There are many examples of situations in which we continue to do things we don't want to do.

- Staying in a job that no longer challenges us
- Staying in a relationship that no longer rewards us
- Avoiding conflict by not telling family we abhor their consumerist lifestyle
- Working long hours without overtime pay because that is what is expected
- Visiting in-laws regularly because it 'keeps the peace'
- Taking all our holidays with our partner because others would think our marriage was in trouble if we didn't

Exercise 18

Look back at Exercise 16 and outline the price you are paying for continuing to do something in your life that you really don't want to do. Write down as much detail as you can to add up the cost of accepting things as they are.

Whatever example you gave, there is a big price to be paid for denying your freedom. This probably includes:

- time and effort involved
- emotional strain
- financial cost
- physical discomfort
- anxiety and resentment
- conflict and argument.

Let us return to our example of work, since it is the structure through which so many of us realise our goals. Take the example of an accountant who stays in a job she doesn't like. Why does she continue to do this? There are many reasons:

- She feels she ought to please others
- She has already made a large investment in terms of time and effort
- She won't admit she trained for this career because the family thought she ought to, instead of pursuing her heart's desire
- She feels it is her duty to provide for others
- She would let her colleagues down
- *Who would she be if she didn't have her job?*

You are not going to live forever. You have limited time in which to make choices. Whatever choice you make, you have to pay the price for what you do by foregoing other alternatives. Therefore, it only makes sense to choose things that will satisfy your very highest values and *let the others go*.

The Dilemma of Change

It is quite amazing in the western world, where we operate under systems of supply and demand, that we don't realise we can change many things as long as we are willing to pay the price. In many aspects of our lives we are able to obtain things we want by paying a price for them, such as buying a house or car. However, when it comes to realising the full extent of our choices, we don't understand that we can choose the life we want to live, *only* if we are prepared to pay the price for it.

It is important to know what you are giving up in the process, the cost of doing so, and ensuring you are not overlooking important things you must give up. In this way there can be no regrets. However, we never stop to evaluate the costs and benefits of obtaining what we want, so we live with the anxiety of 'what if...'

A good example of this is the concept of what we call Career. From a very young age, we are sold the concept of developing skills, experience and expertise which will form part of a longer, integrated path of work during our lives. We talk of career development, career change, changing career direction. We talk of the career as if it is something tangible and real and which can be managed, adapted, re-shaped and re-defined. However, it doesn't exist as a tangible, objective thing in its own right. It is purely a psychological construct by which we build a theme from training, experience, tasks, learning and meaning. In this way, we make sense of the choices we have made, believing that all of them contribute to some ultimate goal. Usually this goal is one of bolstering our self-image and reinforcing a view of ourselves that 'we are getting somewhere.' This is constantly reinforced in our social milieu when one of the first questions we are asked is, 'What do you do for a living?'

Thus, we often give away our power when we attribute meaning and substance to our jobs in defining who we are. When we lose our job, retire or are no longer able to work, we experience enormous anxiety as we grapple with the bigger question of 'who am I without my job title?' Furthermore, we stay in jobs and careers that no longer challenge us. We feel stifled and flat and believe we have no choice. We feel we are an observer in our own lives. However, you are only trapped if you *assume there is no way out*. You must realise that there is a big cost of staying in a job for *fear of what you will lose* rather than *excitement over what you can gain*. There is a way out but there will be a price to pay. This will be in terms of the upheaval, money and emotional anxiety.

Part of the reason people don't even consider change is the vagueness of the situation. The cost is seen as too troublesome to contemplate, so they ignore it and don't think about it directly. They continue to live in the career myth, feeling trapped, and never knowing what it would require to get out. If you knew what was involved and what you were paying to stay and what it would cost to leave, then you could make a definite choice. You would know that the alternative was really best for you. Let me give you an example from my own experience.

Example

Twenty years ago, I had been successfully working as an occupational psychologist for over twelve years. The work took me to many different countries and was well paid. Despite the initial challenge and reinforcement concerning my own ability, I always had a feeling within myself that this wasn't really what I wanted to do. Much of my work was in a corporate environment where it often involved values that were alien to me and I did work that compromised my own values. Many of the values about Western psychology assume a scientific treatment of behaviour, with people being comprised of measurable and comparable traits, abilities and qualities. Conformity to social and occupational norms is seen as desirable and inevitable.

Fear kept me from changing my situation. The reasons I gave myself for maintaining the status quo were related to the earlier investment of time, effort, finance and commitment. I felt successful and valued for my work and wondered who I would be were I not a psychologist. However, the internal conflict became too much as I asked myself the question, 'Who will I be if I am no longer a psychologist?' However, the more pressing question came back, 'Who will you be if you continue to be a psychologist?'

I have always held strong beliefs in the complexity of the human condition and of choice in defining who we are. Traditional scientific approaches focus on the measurement of fixed characteristics and the inevitable external influences to which the majority of us conform. I strongly believed that there was more to this picture. My own views were in contradiction to the very basis on which I was being asked to do my job. I spent several years doing things merely to furnish my CV with evidence of my growth and continued expertise. I engaged in work that I didn't fully enjoy but that I felt would keep me marketable.

I had a choice – to continue with the safe, predictable image I had of myself and hide myself behind my professionalism – or someone else's view of what is professional – or relinquish the role and live with the anxiety of something new. Not just a new job but also a completely different image of who I was. I made that choice. I started to become more outspoken, particularly about ethical leadership, and how wrong it is to pursue profit at any cost. I was also a vegan and wanted to speak out more to wide audiences about the ethical imperative of this. Changing has not been without its costs and anxiety, but it has given me a freedom and sense of well-being that would not have been possible had I not made that change. I had to learn to live with a completely different self-image and set of questions as to who I was without my job. I could no longer hide behind my professionalism or the belief that the work I did somehow contributed to something more real and tangible called 'career.' However, I was embracing my freedom and exploring who I really wanted to be and feeling more purpose and direction.

I am always amazed by the inability of people to realise the traps they have created for themselves and which they perpetuate. Consider the powerful influence that organisations allegedly impose on people regarding working hours. Increasingly, people work longer and longer hours because it is necessary, desirable or inevitable. They complain about the long hours but continue to work them and engage in all sorts of behaviour to establish some sense of balance. Holidays and weekends are eagerly awaited; colleagues are thought of as crazy if they ring into the office on their day off. However, at the same time it is considered valuable to be part of the culture that does this. In the same breath, people admonish others who do work on their laptop whilst on holiday, feel compelled to stay in the office long after the boss has gone in order to show commitment. They never stop to question this contradiction. When challenged, they laugh, saying, 'Well that's just the way things are around here.' Remember, no-one can make you do things you don't want to do without your permission. You have choice and freedom but must be willing to pay the price.

How do you change your life and carve out the life you want to live? You can use the example of changing career but remember that this can be applied to any circumstance in which you find yourself.

Beginning the Process of Change

Take 30 minutes out from your regular routine and find a place that is comfortable and private where you will not be disturbed. Think of the undesirable situation in your life and consider it to be a cage or a prison. Take a paper and pencil with you and complete the following exercise.

Exercise 19

1. Identity the nature of the prison.
   - What is the nature of the problem?
   - What feelings, thoughts and sensations accompany your thinking about the problem?
   - What are you doing in your life at present that causes you discomfort?

2. What would happen if you were no longer in your prison?
   - You might experience the absence of discomfort.
   - You might see the problem as preventing you from having or doing what you want.

3. What if the prison were gone completely?
   - New possibilities arise immediately from the removal of anxiety.
   - One free activity might lead to another.

4. Identify the price that would be incurred to get you out of your prison.
   - It may entail conflict and confrontation.
   - You might feel ashamed.
   - You might lose a friendship.
   - You might be fired.
   - It might take you time to re-establish your reputation of honesty.
   - Others might accuse you of being selfish.
   - Your partner may hate you.
   - Change in self-image.
   - Sense of letting others down.
   - The sense of loss and pain.

5. Picture yourself paying the price.
   - Identify what you have to do to end your present discomfort and then picture yourself paying the price. This may be very difficult, but try.
   - If conflict is entailed, try to imagine how the conversation with the other person would go. Construct an imaginary conversation and outline what each person would say.
   - Imagine what emotions and reactions you would experience. Go over it in your head and live each moment. Try to foresee unexpected reactions of yourself and others. What if the other person becomes abusive or begins to cry?

By doing this exercise, you will have identified:

- How much it is costing you to stay where you are
- What it will cost you to get out
- What to do once you are out

As long as the costs and benefits of change constitute a hazy problem with no solution, it is easier to remain where you are. Once the cost is identified and what you could do if you get out, you will gain new incentive to do something about it. Once identified, the power held by the fear will be reduced. I can hear you saying:

- It just isn't possible to make such big changes by calmly sitting down and mapping out the changes I desire.
- How could I live with the guilt and anxiety that would result?
- What if I regret the decision I have made?
- How could I be so selfish?
- How can I be sure it will work?

- Maintaining the status quo must be right if everyone else is doing it.

It is very important to appreciate that making a decision intellectually is only part of the process of change. In order to make practical changes, you also have to emotionally commit to the change and be prepared to live with the anxiety that uncertainty and resistance from others brings. If you make hasty changes without a fundamental emotional shift from within, you will be tempted to rush back to what you knew before.

Therefore, changing the way you conduct your life begins with testing out small changes. Start with small changes and experience the thrill and anxiety this brings. You can then gradually build up to bigger changes in your life. The role of psychology and counselling is invaluable here since it allows you to make changes in a supportive environment and live through the resultant anxiety and pain in a manageable way. Successful counselling is based on the premise of fundamental personal change in one's experience of being. Thus, if the changes you want to make will require major changes in how you and others see you, seek out the help of a supportive counsellor or psychologist. However, at this stage, choose something minor that you want to change and go through the stages set out above. This will prepare you for the bigger changes in your life.

Exercise 20

Think of something in your life that you would like to change. This should be manageable, like telling your partner you no longer wish to accompany them to see their family every weekend, or telling your boss you feel unappreciated. Work through the following stages, providing as much information as possible at each stage. Identify the nature of the prison:

- What would it be like if you were no longer in the prison?

- What would it be like if the prison were gone completely?
- What price would you have to pay to get out of the prison?
- Imagine yourself paying the price and work through this until it loses its emotional potency.

By experiencing the conflict and confrontation within yourself before you initiate a change, you will be much more prepared to deal with any surprises or unanticipated reactions in yourself and others. If you become afraid and tempted to give in, you can remind yourself of the rewards awaiting if you leave the prison. Remember all the good things you could choose to do with the time you salvage.

For many people, the anticipation of conflict with others is so enormous that they prefer not to make change. However, by staying where you are, you will also experience conflict. You are in fact choosing to live either with the conflict arising from others' reactions, or conflict and unhappiness from doing and thinking about things that just don't contribute to your happiness. If you can make that shift and disappoint another to be true to yourself you will eventually, if not immediately, have a lighter feeling and feel as if a burden has been removed. This may be more difficult for some people than others. Actually, the underlying problem is not the reactions of others but handling the anxiety the situation arouses in us.

Example

A young woman came to me expressing considerable anxiety and conflict. Alison was getting married within the next three months and her partner had just discovered that she had been married before. Her partner, Robert, had been looking forward to marrying in a large Catholic church in Europe.

The plans had been made and the invitations distributed. However, Alison's recent disclosure meant this was not permissible since this was her second marriage. Alison became very distressed as Robert threatened to leave her for her lying, questioning whether there was deceit in other areas of their relationship.

Alison was deeply distressed, knew that she was lying but was unclear as to how she could have divulged this information without the risk of losing Robert. She just feared the confrontation should Robert find out that she had been married before. For her, it was easier to lie, despite the risk that the truth would come out in the end.

Here is an example of someone being unable to handle the anxiety that potential conflict brings. However, there was a cost to not being able to do this. For her, the anxiety was temporarily alleviated as conflict was deferred. However, it arose again when the truth came to light.

In working with Alison, it was important to identify the purpose of lying in her life. Lying had become a very valuable tool to alleviate stress and anxiety, and the reduction in internal conflict served as a powerful negative reinforcer. In this way, her lying can be seen to have a very positive value. She could only give up her lying when she found a way to handle the anxiety that other people's reactions aroused in her.

Therefore, whatever discomfort and anxiety we may feel in facing choices, there is always a price to pay to get rid of it. Many people think that the price of changing is too great, since enormous investment has been made in whatever it is they want to change.

They stay in a job they dread because of the years of investment and training and take the attitude that having endured the discomfort for so long, leaving the situation would mean their anxiety was wasted. If this is the case in your life, try to take a different attitude – you don't have to endure the discomfort any longer. Why spend even more time and distress just because of past wasted time?

Take the example of someone enrolling for a program of study. Halfway through the course, they realise that the subject matter no longer stimulates them and they cannot envisage using the skills or knowledge arising out of the program. The wise thing to do at this point is to cut their losses and leave the program. However, this is often the last thing people do. They weigh up the time spent on the course so far, the financial outlay and the 'opportunity cost' of the past months or years. They soldier on and complete the program, hating every moment of it and wishing for the time when the ordeal will be over. All this they do whilst saying, 'I have spent this much time and effort so far, I am not going to waste it!' However, the time and effort has already been wasted. Instead of salvaging it, they choose to waste even more of their precious time and effort continuing the program. It is true that you can't get the wasted time and money back, but you can get the equivalence back by using the time now to do something you *really* want to do.

I appreciate how hard this can be for many people. Of course, if you have just spent two years and eleven months on a program which has one month to run, it may be wise to complete the next four weeks if achievement of the program would increase your available options. However, if you are only halfway through and you are only completing it because you have a notion that others may value it at some time in the future, alarm bells should be ringing in your head. Choosing the life you want to live means embracing your life and choosing how you want to spend your very precious, limited time. This entails challenging the Commitment Myth.

The same thing applies to things you own. If you have things you no longer need, like or want, sell them! People have attics full of things that they have not looked at for twenty years. Like outdated beliefs, they hold on to these items 'just in case' they will be useful at some time in the future. This time rarely comes and they are left with clutter and are unable to realise the value of the item at all. By giving the items away or converting them into cash, you benefit financially as well as feeling emotionally lighter. You create more space, gain the appreciation of others who can put the item to use, or you can use the cash to buy something you *really* want. Remember that holding on to things that might be useful invariably reflects a reluctance to change outdated beliefs and values that no longer serve you well.

So remember to look at the price you pay every time you notice a discomfort arising from doing something you don't want to do. Find out what it would take to get rid of it. There is *always* a way. If the price is too big to be worth it, think about it some more and perhaps you'll find there is an easier way. Once you consider the price, any irritant in life can be handled. You don't have to tolerate the slow, gnawing discomfort that eats away at you, destroying your incentive, making you like yourself less and becoming cynical. Develop this talent for making choices and evaluating costs. By practicing change on smaller actions and decisions, you can move on to bigger decisions and traps in your life and deal with them in the same way. A sense of well-being and the knowledge of a life being well-lived is the prize for exercising these choices, such as changing your lifestyle or leaving your job.

Remember that as soon as you pay a price, it costs you less. The longer it continues, you pay a price even higher, knowing that it is continuing and is unresolved. Others reinforce you for maintaining the status quo and it becomes even more difficult to change. The sooner you see your mistakes and pay the price quickly, the less interest accumulates on what you are paying.

When making changes, always concentrate on direct alternatives. You may become resentful at the unresolved conflict in your life and blame someone else for your predicament. In an effort to resolve the problem, you spend your time and effort in trying to change this person. You implore your boss to give you more challenging projects, you encourage your partner to be more reasonable. This is a poor use of your time and effort. Instead, evaluate the cost and pay the price to change the situation. To continue with a situation which compromises your needs and values is the real price you have to pay.

Finding Freedom in a Direct Way

It seems that people always look in the wrong direction for freedom. They want political and social change and so focus their efforts on political activity and debate. Kierkeggard said:

> *People hardly ever make use of the freedom which they have, for example, freedom of thought; instead they demand freedom of speech as a compensation.*[13]

They complain about crime or cultural limitations or the rights of minorities. It may be very admirable to be concerned about the wider community in which we live. However, to spend your time and efforts in changing others in order to realise your freedom is really a fruitless exercise. All the time you do this you miss the point of freedom. Accept that everything you do is a choice. You can either meaningfully choose in the knowledge of the responsibility this entails and the anxiety that rejecting the alternatives entails. Alternatively, you can blame others for your limited options and 'choose not to choose.'

People continue to live according to Myths, which serve to reduce the freedom they can experience at this very moment. You can remove the chains within your own reach. The reality is that by embracing your own freedom, you act as an example and catalyst for others to do the same. The greatest love and concern for others is often discipline: by putting yourself first in your life, you mirror to them that real freedom comes from living a more authentic life *now*.

Exercise 21

What could you do today to give you more freedom tomorrow morning?

Breaking Your Own and Others' Commitment Myth

The Commitment Myth is that it is impossible to change certain things in our lives once we have committed to them. How can you avoid the Commitment Myth ruling your life and point it out in others?

- Recognise that freedom is your responsibility and it is only the enormity of this responsibility that causes anxiety and prevents you from enjoying it.
- Take responsibility for your choices and don't blame other people, society or social norms for not exercising them.
- Choose things that will satisfy your highest values and let the others go.
- Recognise that you can change almost anything in your life as long as you are prepared to pay the price involved in the transaction.
- Examine all your activities very closely and ensure that you are not doing things, even in your leisure time, that serve to bolster a self-image that others have chosen for you.

- See undesirable situations in your life as prisons. By identifying the nature of the prison, the implications of leaving it and the price you will pay for your departure, you will have a clearer picture of the costs involved in staying and the benefits to be gained from leaving.
- Real change occurs when you emotionally commit to doing things differently. By mentally working through the price of change, you can anticipate and prepare for the reactions of yourself and others.
- Test out small changes and work towards the bigger changes in your life. The assistance of a therapist or mentor may be necessary to handle the anxiety which arises out of making the bigger changes.
- Remember that the only way to gain the equivalence of resources wasted so far is to use your time, money and efforts exactly how you want to *now*.
- Don't try to change the world. Embrace the freedom you have now and see the additional benefit of acting as an example and catalyst for change in others.

Chapter 6

The Certainty Myth

There is an enduring rightness in our decisions that lead us to a point beyond which we don't need to look any further.

Anxiety – the Cost of Meaningful Living

Existential philosophy is often blamed for being overly negative and focused on issues of death and anxiety. Surely, in an uncertain world, we would want to avoid such discomfort and make sense of the human condition?

R.D. Laing believed that the schizophrenic experience was one of ontological insecurity whereby the individual cannot take their identity for granted and has a fear that their very self will be annihilated. Van Deurzen criticized Laing, saying that ontological insecurity is not the experience of the schizophrenic alone but all of us who must face the reality of uncertainty and finitude.

Whilst we may not question our very existence on a daily basis, our attempts to avoid uncertainty and change might indicate our desire to avoid the anxiety associated with our impermanent nature. This only causes more anxiety in the long run. Van Deurzen-Smith says:

> *Some people succeed in living in an anxiety-free state, mechanically moving along with the ever-returning duties of daily life. They pretend to themselves that life is just this way and that they themselves are made the way they are, without there being anything that they can do about it. When there are no options, there is no anxiety.*

> *As soon as people are aware of the basic choices that life involves them in they are condemned to the experience of anxiety.*[14]
>
> Thus, anxiety is an inevitable cost of living a meaningful life. To engage with the reality of our limited time invites us to examine our choices for happiness.

It is a common belief that we have similar experiences to others, since much of our time and activities are spent with them. However, our experiences are unique, and whilst the circumstances surrounding them may be similar to those of others, they are fundamentally different.

De Beauvoir talks of the concept of 'Fundamental Ambiguity,' where an individual experiences their life as 'inwardness' – the unfolding of a story visible only to them. Each individual is also aware of the same life in terms of externality. Others have their memories of you from their external perspective, as you remember your past from an internal one. You cannot give a fixed, objective meaning to your own life – others recall events from their own perspectives and perceive you differently as a result. Thus, we are not fixed entities but created through interaction with other people. De Beauvoir says that people who cannot live with *fundamental ambiguity* become oppressive and authoritarian and cannot allow others to tolerate their truth. What does she mean by this? Presumably she is highlighting that there is no objective rightness in making sense of our lives and that our perception of ourselves and others is always a function of who is experiencing it.

With this is mind, many of us try to live our lives as if it were possible to achieve some objective understanding of the world. Likewise, there is a tendency for us to act as if it were possible to gain complete information on which we can make decisions. We would like to believe that there is a certain rightness in our decisions because somewhere 'out there' there is an objective purpose or set of information that would confirm those decisions. This is a Myth and is based on the belief that the assumptions on which we make decisions are certain. There is a real desire by all of us to seek out what we believe to be 'the truth' so that we can be spared the risk that goes with all decisions.

This is not possible. All of our decisions are based on assumptions. These assumptions may be based on a large amount of information or experience but they are *still* assumptions and are based on beliefs, perceptions, and hunches, values – all of which are changeable. Consider the enormous benefit in this. We can change our beliefs, values and hunches in the light of new information and experience.

It would, of course, be very comfortable if we could be certain about our decisions and how they will affect us now and in the future. Observe others around you and see what lengths they go to, to reinforce the notion of certainty. Social and cultural norms serve to provide a sense of stability and predictability. They are powerful determinants of behaviour and reinforcers of certainty. However powerful they may be, they are continually socially and individually challenged and the resultant change reflects further uncertainty and change.

Exercise 22

Reflect on your life and outline the things you do regularly that make you feel it is certain and predictable. This may relate to a daily routine or may be more far-reaching in terms of some religious or mystical belief.

Looking for Certainty

Some people engage in religious activity believing that there is an objective authority outside of themselves which preordains how things should be. Others develop elaborate routines in their lives to increase a sense of predictability and control. People act through an imposed sense of duty, believing that there is a rightness in how they should act. Organisations create clearly defined role definitions so that jobholders know what is expected of them and others will be clear about the parameters of their responsibilities. They develop their own cultures which also provide a sense of shared experience and prediction. Whilst culture is undoubtedly a major determinant of behaviour, it is a Myth that this means certainty. Morgan says that organisational culture creates an illusion of certainty which detracts from the bigger concern of uncertainty. He says of organisations that:

> *...they encourage us to understand many of our symbolic acts and constructions as flights from our own mortality. In joining with others in the creation of culture as a set of shared norms, beliefs, ideas and social practices, we attempt to locate ourselves in something large and more enduring than ourselves.*[15]

Thus organisational reality creates and sustains a perception of permanence and solidity as an instrument of what Sartre calls Bad Faith. If the individual conforms to this notion of reality, they are, in effect, denying their ultimate freedom and choice since they are denying the inevitable reality that such ideals only exist as long as individuals want this to be so – not because of an objective rightness for all time.

All these activities are based on assumptions grounded in the Certainty Myth. To have a feeling of absolute certainty is unrealistic. You only have a fraction of the information you would need to make a decision with complete foresight. However, we often act on information as if it were complete and objective, only to find later that this was not and can never be the case. Consider the following examples:

- We buy a house, believing that this will be the place in which we will spend the rest of our lives. At the time of buying, the house was seen as the perfect home of which we have always dreamed. It is in a desirable neighbourhood, is spacious and accessible to activities we regularly engage in. However, several years later, we find that our neighbours cause us so many problems that we can't understand how we could have moved there in the first place.
- You are offered a new job. It seems like a dream job, offering you the promise of moving from your existing role, which is highly demanding and set within a political minefield. You say that you can't believe your luck and that you can never imagine leaving it. However, a short time into the job, a jealous colleague, who considers you are encroaching on their patch, threatens the certainty of your role. Suddenly the dream job has become a nightmare.
- You enter a new relationship, believing this to be 'the one' which will last a lifetime. You compare it to past relationships and are gripped with the overwhelming sense of rightness of your decision to be with the other person. The feeling is so overwhelming that you state, with complete certainty, that you will 'always' be

> together. Three years down the line, you rethink your decision and consider that you might be better off on your own.

The previous three examples indicate how a feeling of rightness in our decisions 'at the time' may be translated to 'rightness for all time.' An overwhelming feeling of certainty *at one time* is just that – it doesn't mean that it will feel that way or turn out that way for all time. This is because we cannot be certain about the thoughts, expectations, motivations and actions of others. Also, we cannot be sure how 'we' will act, think or feel about things in light of information to which we did not previously have access.

However, this does not mean that we cannot make decisions and act on them. Appreciate that all things are uncertain and that information and knowledge to hand is always incomplete and that, in the light of new information (currently not available), you may want to change your plans or ideas. This inherent uncertainty in everything you do should not stop you from acting. If you can recognise and accept the inherent ambiguity in everything in life, you will appreciate the purpose of the uncertainty. Uncertainty constitutes the risks involved in what you do. The risks equal the liability or price you will pay if things don't go as you want them to.

It is important that you accept that, in all decisions, there is a risk, — the price you will be called upon to pay if things don't work out as planned. In the above examples, the price to be paid included such things as loss of face, pride, frustration, lost equity, upheaval, unhappiness, stress, and pain. The potential price has to be paid regardless of how certain you felt your choice to be. However, it is likely to be higher if you invested your time, financial and emotional resources into the decision because you believed the outcome would be certain for all time. The emotional cost is likely to be particularly high, since your basic assumptions and beliefs about certainty are also likely to be challenged. Living with the anxiety of 'not knowing' and 'not being certain' can be difficult and challenging but can offer you a greater sense of freedom in a number of ways:

- You will not take risks that are unacceptable or which could get you into commitments or boxes that would be unacceptable. These commitments could constitute an undesirable marriage, business opportunities, limiting beliefs or more seriously, suicide pacts; common in religious sects.
- When things don't work out the way you had wished, you will not be plunged into despair and depression. If you have invested all your resources and dreams into something because of a certainty in its rightness, your very assumptions and beliefs on which you base your life – certainty – will be challenged. This can be very distressing and cause you to challenge the very core of who you are rather than focusing on changeable aspects of your experience.
- You will not accept the opinions of others to be absolute facts because they may simply be untrue.

Explaining Uncertainty

In a desire for certainty, we often try to seek out an explanation for everything. Many things happen in our lives, which appear to defy explanation.

Exercise 23

Think of something that has happened in your life which appeared to defy explanation. It may be something short-lived, like the unwelcome behaviour of a friend. It may also be something like news of a terminal illness or death of a child. Outline the detail of the experience and what reasons you attributed to it happening.

When an event happens in our lives which we find difficult to understand, we often search desperately for an explanation or something that will make the event meaningful. Consider the tragic situation where a young child dies of a terminal illness. Those witnessing this event respond differently to the news. How could this happen to a child so young? What is the purpose of this? How can life be so unfair? Several different explanations may be sought.

For example:

- It was god's will.
- He was an old spirit - it was his time to go.
- She must have done something bad in a previous life.
- He died of cancer but never smoked! There is therefore no link between smoking and cancer.
- There is no meaning to life – I am not going to bother anymore.
- I won't love anyone again – I always lose the people I love.
- There must be a greater order to life – I know I will see her again.

All of these responses are highly individualised, based on each individual's assumptions and beliefs. However, to turn them into certain explanations as to why the child died at so young an age is to avoid the anxiety of living with uncertainty. This only causes more anxiety in the long run. Van Deurzen-Smith says:

> *Existential anxiety or Angst is that basic unease or malaise which people experience as soon as they are aware of themselves. It is the sensation which accompanies self-consciousness and awareness of one's vulnerability when confronted with the possibility of one's death. It is therefore the sine qua*

> *non of facing life and finding oneself.*
>
> *Anxiety can only be temporarily eliminated by plunging oneself deeply into existence in a mindless way. By living as if one were like an object, solid and predetermined, existential anxiety can be postponed until the time when this fake certainty is proven false. As soon as awareness of the fundamental lack of substance and security of the human condition is reached one is again exposed to the bare reality of existence which evokes anxiety.*[16]

Thus, anxiety is an inevitable cost of living a meaningful life. To a large extent, Van Deurzen-Smith is talking about the ultimate anxiety regarding our finitude and death. To engage with the reality of our limited time invites us to examine our choices for happiness. She goes on to say:

> *...the people who try hardest to deny the realities of life will also be those who will be most forcefully reminded of their own limitations. They who run from their inner anxieties will experience the stalled anxiety even more acutely later.*[17]

The search for explanations may be a fruitless exercise or may cause us to take foolish action or develop beliefs and attitudes that don't serve us well. Consider the following explanations for certain life experiences.

- I was fired because my boss doesn't like women. I will never again apply for a management job where there isn't a woman on the board.
- A friend of mine died whilst on a motorbike so I will never get on one again.

- I was bitten by a dog when a young child – I would never have a companion animal now.
- We all eat animal products and if it was so bad, then why is everyone doing it?

It also happens with certain mystical experiences where we cannot live with the uncertainty of not knowing objectively what the purpose of life is all about.

- I cannot explain how the universe was created and therefore there must be a god.
- When I am ready for a relationship, the universe will just bring one along.
- God is in command so I don't have to take responsibility for my actions.

All these explanations, and others, may be adopted just because we don't have the answer at the time. This is not to denigrate a person's religious beliefs. However, accepting that uncertainty is a 'reality' allows us to live with more passion – focusing on the value of our lives and the choices that face us. Our beliefs then reflect a direct choice rather than an inevitable outcome of responding in a way we believe is appropriate.

Exercise 24

Think of a time in your life when something happened to you where you became anxious or fearful. It may be the loss of a job, which made you more anxious about financial security. It may be the loss of a close friendship, which made you more anxious about trusting others. Write down as much information as possible about the event and the feelings and anxieties, which it provoked.

Living with Anxiety

Often things happen in our lives which make us acutely aware of our own vulnerability. Although the perceived threat or anxiety was always potentially there, we may not have been aware of it and so never considered it. We may have theoretically considered what it was like to 'run out of money' but it was never considered to be a real threat. Then something happens which brings this concern to the fore and we are overwhelmed with anxiety and fear of what the future holds.

Example

A client developed a repetitive strain injury in her left hand. This proceeded to extend up towards the shoulder and then the identical condition developed in her right arm. This young woman found the most rudimentary tasks, like brushing her hair, painful and distressing events. To be left without the use of one's arms and hands is to reappraise every aspect of one's life. To not be able to feed oneself or care for one's basic needs is a terrifying experience. It has major practical, emotional and social implications.

My client couldn't perform simple tasks like feeding, washing or dressing herself without extreme pain. She felt worthless and her identity as a strong woman who had overcome major obstacles in her life was challenged. Suddenly she was dependent on the care of others. She became fearful that her husband and friends would tire of her, and so avoided making her fears known. As a result, she felt more lonely and isolated. She began to challenge her spiritual beliefs, asking, 'How could God do this to me?' She perceived the world to be highly unpredictable and fretted about how she could financially make ends meet if she was no longer able to work.

In therapy, we explored these very deeply-felt fears. After many sessions, we did not appear to be making any progress towards accessing resources to deal with them. For her, life was now so unpredictable that it was not worth going on. Over time, certain issues were explored around the notion of uncertainty and I made the following comment:

'I was wondering if the underlying fears you express are ones we must all face as human beings from time to time? Perhaps we all feel that things are unpredictable and wonder how we might meet our financial obligations? Maybe everyone we come into contact with has fears, which arise as we ask:

- Will I be loved?
- Am I any good at what I do?
- Will I be able to pay my bills?
- Will I become so down that I won't be able to pick myself up?

In your case, the reality is that these potential fears have always been there. It is just that your physical injury has brought them to the fore. This is the very anxiety of living – we live in an uncertain world, made more uncertain by the changing actions, thoughts, and beliefs of others. The only certainty we can have is some belief in our ability to be open to the ebbs and flows of life and live with the anxiety of our own vulnerability. That is the very essence of what it is to be human.'

These concepts were explored over many months and gradually my client began to see things a little differently and appreciate that her anxiety pointed to a more fundamental questioning of meaning and purpose. This is when therapy took a new direction for her.

To engage with our freedom is to accept that certainty is only a Myth. Accept the experiences that you have as just that – you don't have to change the world because things appear unpredictable. They are! Don't allow this reality to force you to pursue concrete explanations for everything that happens, and be open enough to live with the anxiety of not knowing. Don't expect that everything has an explanation. It may come to light later but, in the meantime, live with the ambiguity of this wonderful experience called Living.

Sometimes things that highlight our vulnerability can be seen as valuable, since they alert us to the possibility of threat or danger in our lives.

Example

A week before I emigrated to Australia from the UK, I was approached by a distressed young woman asking for my help. She had apparently been locked out of her home and was asking for some small change in order to make a telephone call. The event happened directly outside my home, and as her stance was non-threatening, I considered her plea to be genuine. However, when I removed my purse from my bag, she leapt forward and snatched my purse. I never saw her again.

My reaction over the next few days was interesting. I felt used and embarrassed by the event. After all, I had willingly retrieved my purse from my handbag and made the theft easy for her. I admonished myself, saying, 'How could I be so naïve?' The event seemed even more terrible to me since she had appealed to me, as a neighbour, to help her as a vulnerable individual. I felt abused and realised also that suddenly the world no longer felt safe, particularly as the event happened outside my home. For weeks after, I was cautious when returning home, walking in the centre of the road to my house to avoid the dark shadows.

> Then one day I reflected on my behaviour and realised that, in fact, the threat of being mugged had always been there. The cynic might say that I had been lucky to live in London for twenty years and not be mugged! The threat had always been there – it was just that now it had come into my consciousness.
>
> It was at this point that I was able to learn from the event. I reflected on the fact that sometimes I am naïve and trust unknowingly. This could put me in a position of unnecessary vulnerability.
>
> The event taught me to be more cautious and protective of my safety. There was only 17 pounds in my purse – what a wonderful lesson to learn – and it only cost me 17 pounds!

The previous example shows how we can learn and benefit from engaging with the reality of uncertainty and vulnerability. The more we can trust our ability to deal with the anxiety of uncertainty, the more we can engage with the process of living. However, many of us caught in the Certainty Myth seek the advice and information of others. We often accept as certain, knowledge from others which is subject to the human limits of perception and error. Consider the many people of your parents' era who slavishly believed the judgement of the doctor – many to the detriment of their lives. This is not to undermine the value of the medical profession, but to blindly accept with certainty another's viewpoint as if it cannot be challenged is an example of the Certainty Myth.

Remember that people see things through their own eyes and yet we often accept what they say as verbatim truth. This is due to the Certainty Myth. Consider religious scholars who believe in the word of God in the Bible as if it were verbatim. However, the Bible, whether or not it was inspired by God, was written by fallible interpreters who were expressing their understanding of what they believed to be true. This does not devalue its content – it means that the reading of such texts should be done with an open mind and challenged in the light of new information.

It is the same in many walks of life. When we believe in the claims of others, they may be misinterpreting the causes of their own success, and the techniques they used may not produce the same effects when we use them.

Looking to Others for Answers

There are, indeed, many sources of information that help us learn and from which we may take advice. Books, films, ideas, and suggestions offer sources of inspiration to help stimulate our search for our own truth. Likewise, the concepts in this book should themselves be challenged and questioned. Do not accept these as absolute, final answers to problems or the mysteries of life or else you are only living the Certainty Myth. Consider the power which we may give to those people who are considered 'expert' in their own field.

Exercise 25

Think of a time in your life when you accepted the advice of an expert to be sound and certain. Outline the nature of the advice and what action you took as a result of it.

Often people over-respect the judgement of someone who appears to have mastered a body of knowledge and has gone through lengthy training. It appears that these experts have insight and expertise outside our range of experience. This may be in the form of a wise grandfather whom people listen to because of his years of experience. It is true that this person has lived many years but this, in itself, does not constitute wisdom. The seventy-year-old may have had many years of experience and developed a certain degree of wisdom. However, since adulthood, he might have had one year's worth of experience 52 times because he has lived a life which has been deliberately sheltered from the anxiety of living with uncertainty and openness to others' ideas.

The label of 'expert' is often given to those professionals who have the status that attributes to them certain expertise, separate from the rest of us.

Example

Having completed a lengthy training and supervision period, I worked as a psychologist in London for several years. I provided advice to a client on aspects of their human resource management. I remember sitting in a board meeting advising the directors as to how they should deal with an aspect of change that was going to impact on every individual in the organisation. A particular phrase comes to mind. They said, 'Thank you for your advice. Based on it, we think we will move in this direction. However, if, at any time, you advise us to take a different direction, we will, of course, bow to your expert knowledge.'

I remember leaving that meeting thinking, 'I believe I have given them the best advice I could, based on my knowledge and expertise. However, I do think these managers should take responsibility here – surely they know the business better than I do since they work there all the time? In this and later decisions, this is an unreasonable relinquishing of responsibility. Also, what happens if they take my advice and it all goes wrong, since I only have limited information?'

Individuals and organisations regularly give this kind of power to experts. Often we rely on others for information as we cannot do everything in the limited time we have. However, information providers often make mistakes because, like us, they are constantly faced with new information which they didn't originally have to hand at the time of making a decision or giving advice.

Any expert's advice is underpinned by a set of values and assumptions which they have chosen to adopt. However, often those values are part and parcel of the wider group or professional body to which they belong. If they want to continue to practice and be respected, they must adhere to the values and ways of working that stem from it – even if they don't totally agree. Thus, the expert may end up giving advice which they themselves question. It is as if they have a hammer and every problem becomes a nail!

Therefore, use caution in acting upon information given by others. Consider the advice given by a doctor. One doctor says one thing and another disputes it. Years of experience and schooling cannot provide them with an insurance against human fallibility and personal judgement.

Each of us is good at different things and constantly looks for advice and information from more knowledgeable others when making decisions. Do not accept the advice of another as certain just because it came from someone labelled 'expert.' This means that we must take responsibility for all of our decisions and not point to our advisers when things don't work out as we would have wished. By all means, gather information and appraise others' advice, but to accept it as the objective truth will lead to disappointment. If you do accept their advice, know that this is a choice for now and is open to future modification.

Exercise 26

Outline the factors which you consider influence an expert's ideas. You might like to use an example of you receiving advice from someone you consider to be an expert. Infer from their advice the factors that might have influenced their conclusions. For example, fundamental belief in the body of knowledge in their particular area of expertise.

Many factors influence the advice we give and the perspective of each of us, including experts. Experts are subject to whims, emotional problems, political objectives, hopes for promotion, and vested interests in previously stated opinions. This is normal and predictable. Many a professor's words have been accepted as gospel when they were meant as a joke or backhanded comment taken out of context. Many a researcher prematurely comes to a conclusion because of the demands of a deadline. Given more time, the outcome may have been presented differently.

There is no source which you can look to for ultimate truth and the final answer to anything or everything. Why do we think there is something 'out there' when we cannot even agree what is 'in here'? De Beauvoir's concept of Fundamental Ambiguity is a case in point where each of us experiences our lives uniquely and subjectively.

Therefore, accept an expert's view as opinion and then you can be aware of the risks when you take action on the information. You will be less likely to jump into trouble you cannot handle.

The Myth

The Certainty Myth is that you can disregard the risks by overestimating the certainty of information on which you base your decisions. Taking a risk is a part of life. It is only dangerous if you act as if you are not taking a risk. You are colluding with the Certainty Myth if you base your life on what someone has told you is the way to live, that God commanded it, or when you think your actions will definitely produce certain results.

It is just as foolish to expect someone to act on the basis of your own knowledge. For example, I remember moving to Australia and many people saying, 'You will love it here – it has everything to offer!' Whilst that may have been their experience and later proved to have echoes of mine, it was an unreasonable statement. There were many factors which influenced whether living in Australia would be a positive thing for me. Likewise, in all the decisions you make, do not be swayed by others' opinions of what will definitely be right for you if you take the action they themselves took with their unique set of needs, expectations and circumstances. When you have decided you are sure enough to act on something, you don't need others' approval to confirm it is the right decision. If you do, you are being influenced by the Identity Myth where you expect others to act as you would, given the same knowledge.

Reactions to Things that Happen

It is interesting to observe other people's reactions when things happen in their lives. This provides valuable insight into how they relate to the world.

Van Deurzen-Smith[18] discusses a valuable existential frame of reference for considering an individual's worldview. The first three dimensions stem from earlier writers, e.g. Bingswanger[19]; Boss[20] and the last one she has added herself. They are:

- **Physical Dimension:** the natural world comprising the physical, biological dimension where individuals tend to behave in an instinctual manner.
- **Social Dimension**: the public world comprising human relationships and interactions where individuals tend to behave in a learnt cultured manner.
- **Personal Dimension**: the private world comprising intimate and personal experiences where individuals obtain their sense of identity and ownership.
- **Spiritual Dimension**: the ideal world comprising beliefs and aspirations where individuals relate to values beyond themselves.

The previous framework provides a means of examining our human experience. The following is a simple example of how the dimensions can be valuable in exploring your own experiences.

Example

Imagine a young teenager. He might be ill-at-ease in his body following the rapid change in its shape and reactions. He might be acutely aware of the opposite or same sex and find that he becomes embarrassed and sensitive in his interactions with them. He may also be looking to what are the appropriate ways of responding to people and events. In this respect, his culture and upbringing will influence his beliefs and evaluation of them. He may become more conscious of how his feelings and thoughts about himself are changing and what is consistent. He may also be aware of ideals and aspirations beyond his own self. He may be passionately involved in conservation issues, believing that greater care should be taken of the planet.

This simple example indicates the four dimensions of his experience. His experience of being in his body – the **physical dimension**; his interactions with others and appropriate responses – the **social dimension**; his internal awareness of himself and that he is separate from others – the **personal dimension;** and his ideals and aspirations about conservation – the **spiritual dimension**.

Exploring your own or another's worldview using this framework allows for awareness of the uniqueness and subjectivity of our experiences. It is in sharp contrast to traditional and scientific frameworks which diagnose and categorise personal characteristics with the view of developing norms and comparing them with others. The theme of this book is choice and individual responsibility – such a framework reinforces your uniqueness and personal needs.

Exercise 27

Using Van Deurzen-Smith's four categories, outline factors that have contributed to your current perspective on the freedom and choices you are currently faced with in your life. Provide a short sentence to explain how these factors manifest themselves in your daily life.

- Physical Dimension
- Social Dimension
- Personal Dimension
- Spiritual Dimension

Thus, rather than attributing events and happenings to things like your glands, unreasonable bosses, acts of God or personality attributes, keep an open mind until you are able to make a decision – which you may later change – as to factors that contributed to those events. Your unique worldview can be a valuable way of considering the different aspects of your perceptions. Remember, the risk is always there, you must pay the price and repair the damage, but don't waste your time blaming others, your glands, God's wrath, or foolish resolutions. This is part of being alive and being in the world. Uncertainty is part of living and also makes for change and growth.

When you live by the Certainty Myth you are making yourself very vulnerable. When things do go badly wrong, this is such a contradiction of your attitudes that it may cause you enormous emotional distress. All appears to be lost. In an attempt to recoup a sense of certainty, you may also leap to conclusions which are the opposite of what you believed before. Many a devil worshipper may become a religious zealot, a couch potato; a health fanatic or committed carnist; a vegan activist! The reasonable person appreciates that everything is a gamble.

Taking the risk and responsibility and paying the price if things go wrong starts with not slavishly believing in assumptions which others believe to be correct. In many ways, western culture makes it difficult and undesirable to live with uncertainty. The whole financial and insurance industry implores us to 'take control of our future' as if a policy could offset the reality that the future is unpredictable. True, it might alleviate the experience of anxiety at the time but it will not remove it. Advice abounds on how to secure your business and finances. Certainty even surrounds our personal relationships – the act of marriage is a statement about certainty, which is contradicted by the divorce statistics. A once popular song in the UK entitled 'I knew I loved you before I met you' points to the assumption that somewhere out there, someone is destined for you and in whom you can be certain. The wise person doesn't believe in the myth of Absolute Certainty. They don't believe they have the answer for everything. They are open to life's experiences and if they fall in love, they don't emphatically state that it will be forever. Remember that the world is full of people who made the same statements, only to eat their words in the divorce courts two years later.

Don't let uncertainty stop you from enjoying what you have and don't let overconfidence lead you to act on what you don't yet have.

Summary

Many people go through life believing that they know things because others have decreed it. Professionals or professors claim to be the fount of knowledge in their specialist area. They claim that their profession exists to safeguard the client when an alternative perspective is that it reduces the supply of available advisers and increases the fees they can charge. Professional advice thus becomes a scarce resource for which people pay large sums of money, often for the thin promise of certainty.

People may know many things but not everything about anything or anything about everything. They certainly don't know about you. You are the authority on your own life. You have to judge how new information fits with how you see the world; how the information fits with your values and capabilities and how happy you might be if you adopt them.

There is no authority outside of you that can offer you 100% certainty, regardless of what your spiritual or mystical beliefs may be. How nice if there were – you could delegate your decision in the way that parents try to by taking responsibility for their children or in the way many people expect governmental bodies to control certain areas of their lives.

Probably the closest you can get to a certainty is that you can't decide not to choose! This means real responsibility. You live in a world that is full of your own knowledge and experience.

Many people do what others expect with no real question as to its appropriateness or validity. Many people see heterosexual marriage and children as a normal state of affairs and a certain and mature way of living. When others challenge these 'certain states' by developing 'alternative lifestyles' they are criticised and labelled as abnormal or sick. Fortunately progressive societies are accepting a wider definition of what is acceptable.

Consider the woman who decides not to have children. Cries of 'How selfish' are heard. However, how many people had their own children for the children's sake? The desire to be a parent appears to be so overwhelming that their selfishness is never challenged. One could argue that choosing to have children is a selfish act since it is the parents who want the experience of having children. This is not to denigrate the enormous pleasure that these choices might bring many people. However, when people choose alternative lifestyles or activities contrary to acceptable social norms or life stages, accept it as just that – their choice!

In our search for certainty, society holds up certain acceptable behaviours as the acceptable and normal way of being. Believing that there is a certain, objective world lulls people into a safe life which is believed to exist long after they are gone. My own experience as a psychologist has shown me that when people are on their death bed, the reactions of those who have lived life to the full – regardless of whether it was in their home town or exploring the world – are in stark contrast to those who have chosen the tight confines of assumed certainty. Those who have not lived life to the full are more fearful of death than those who have.

Don't forfeit your freedom and happiness by delegating to others the power that can be used effectively only by yourself. You can be the author of your own life – that is a certainty!

Breaking Your Own and Others' Certainty Myth

The Certainty Myth is that there is an enduring rightness in our decisions. It convinces us that there is an objective reality and if only we can access sufficient knowledge, we can make decisions that are absolutely correct and which will spare us the risk of disappointment. Sadly, this is not the case. However, if we accept this, we can look life squarely in the face, with all its risks, and live our lives meaningfully and to the full.

How can you avoid the Certainty Myth ruling your life and point it out in others?

- Appreciate that there is no objective reality and that you are the creator of your own subjective world.
- Appreciate that all decisions are based on assumptions which arise out of beliefs, perceptions and hunches about information you currently have to hand.

- Accept that absolute certainty is not possible and that living with the anxiety of not knowing the full picture is a part of living.
- Appreciate that a feeling of rightness now does not mean rightness for all time. Be prepared to change your decisions in light of new information.
- Recognise the risks and liabilities. Risks equal the liabilities and prices to be paid if things don't work out as you want them to. Accept this and your losses won't be so critical.
- Accept that your way of explaining things offers you information about your personal way of looking at the world. Explanations are not absolute and objective – they offer you insight into how you see things and who you want to be.
- Appreciate that the world is unpredictable and that living with the unpredictability of life offers the opportunity of living more meaningfully.
- Be cautious of blindly trusting the opinions of experts since they come from decisions based on limited information they have to hand at the time. Instead, use their information to make informed judgements which can change in light of new information.
- Remember that popularity is not proof and what is common knowledge is not absolute reality. Be sceptical about new information and don't expect an explanation for everything.

Chapter 7

The Morality Myth

You should follow a moral code decreed by others.

Does an external morality exist?

At the heart of existential theory is the notion that there is no objective reality and that we are free to create our own way of being and thus our own morality. Sartre[21] reminds us of how difficult this is and so we spend much of our time trying to define our reality and create the illusion that a blueprint exists into which we will fit and are part of.

Sartre says that uncomfortable emotions result from accepting our nothingness and freedom to do and think what we choose. These emotions comprise:

Anguish as life events cause us to challenge our way of being, our values and identity.

Absurdity as we embrace the possibility that everything is dispensable.

Nausea as we realise others are free and therefore challenge our definitions of who we are.

Abandonment as we accept our aloneness and no higher morality deciding our fate.

Despair as we realise there is nothing beyond ourselves.

It is of little surprise therefore that through Bad Faith we attempt to avoid the sense of meaninglessness that is inevitable if we embrace this reality, and that our social structures are adopted to

> create the illusion of permanence, shared morality and objective reality. Thus, with no universal morality or if God does not exist '...there disappears with him, all possibility of finding values in an intelligible heaven.' Sartre[22]

The Morality Myth dictates that your behaviour and actions should be in accordance with a moral code decreed by others. It operates like the Identity Myth in that it requires you to be like other people. It is a powerful form of social control, and sanctions are imposed on those who behave in 'immoral' ways. However, by giving in to those pressures to conform, you are letting yourself be manipulated by others and not choosing the codes by which you want to live your life.

What exactly is morality? It refers to something being either 'right' or 'wrong.' When people do things that are moral, it appears that their actions are in accordance with principles that are right or wrong. But what is right? It is something that is moral! Thus confusion is created in the definition, let alone what it means in reality.

Whose standards are we supposed to conform to in order to be considered right and moral? Let us look at three different types of morality to see if some light can be thrown on this concept:

- Individual morality
- Universal morality
- Absolute morality

Individual Morality

We all behave in ways that will bring about the best consequences for ourselves; those that we believe will make us happy. It may not appear to others that it is bringing about the best consequences for us, but whether we believe it or not, we are the judge of what is best for us at any given time. All our actions will have consequences and we need to be able to take responsibility for them. Some of the consequences are immediately apparent to us whilst others come to light as we go through life. For example, if you want to be rich and give up work, the quickest way would probably be to rob a bank. However, the possibility of getting caught is pretty high. Other actions to bring about this desire may not be so clear.

Exercise 28

Think of a time when you decided on a course of action to bring about a desired outcome. It may have been entering a relationship, starting a business, travelling around the world or deciding to tackle your boss about her bullying management style. Outline the consequences that you were aware of at the time and those that only came to light as you took the action.

There will be many examples that you could have chosen since our lives are full of a myriad of decisions and actions. Let us use the example of how to become financially independent. You might decide to work long hours to save large sums of money. This decision has consequences. Some are clear from the outset: you will have to invest large amounts of time and energy to achieve your goal. This may appear to be an attractive option since, at the time of your decision, you thrive on the stimulation of a full-time, high paying job. However, as time goes on, unforeseen consequences come to the fore. You become tired and jaded – what was a means to an end has become an end in itself and by now your perceived commitments are so high that you no longer consider you have a choice. This is where a personal and individual moral code is important.

You need to have a general rule to help you make decisions. It should be the grounding feature of your life that helps you avoid potential disasters and reminds you of things you do to satisfy your most important long-term desires. Ask yourself, 'How can I get what I want without spoiling my chances of getting other things which, in the long term, are more important to me?' For example, you might find yourself in a romantic encounter which appears attractive and a means to meet your immediate sexual needs. However, your longer-term goal is to find a partner with whom you can form a lasting relationship. You have to decide whether this short-term encounter will interfere with your longer-term goal. Making yourself available for short-term encounters may blind you to the real benefits of finding something that, in the long term, is more important to you.

Thus, your *individual morality should be a generalised, long-term attitude which acts as your code of conduct*. This is the purpose of morality, to help you keep in mind the direction in which *you* want to go. Personal morality relates to the consequences that will affect you. However, how your actions affect others is also important because it directly affects you! Therefore the purpose of deliberately choosing an individual moral code is that it gives you an overall view that will help you find happiness.

You have to develop your own moral code; no one else is qualified to tell you how to live. To be useful, your code should be a general rule to keep you focused on your ultimate goals. It is an attempt to bear in mind all the relevant consequences of your actions.

Example

I recall a time when I became acutely aware of my own moral code. I was living in London and considering the sale of the property I owned and lived in. I accepted an attractive offer by a woman looking forward to owning the property. The next day I was offered 10,000 pounds more by another buyer. I was caught in a dilemma. Should I take the more attractive offer or stand by my word and sell the property to the first buyer? I spent two days pondering this dilemma – arguments like, 'This is business – sentiment shouldn't come into it' weighed in favour of the higher offer. 'The first buyer will be terribly disappointed and I did give her my word' swayed my decision in the opposite direction.

I remember discussing the dilemma with my father, a man whose values and integrity meant he would not question the direction of his decision. He would have stood by his word, regardless of the amount of money involved. Instead of pressing his values on me, he said, 'You have to make your own decision. The best advice I can give you is that you are the only one who can choose what values to live your life by. You can choose to take the extra money or stand by your word. How much is your word worth? Are you prepared to sell it for 10,000 pounds? What happens when another person offers another 10,000 pounds? Will you continue to be swayed every time someone changes the goal posts? If you are, the cost to you will be your loss of control and belief in your own values. If you put your stake in the ground and say, "I will stand by my word" that is one thing you can rely on in a world that constantly changes the goalposts.'

I reflected on his advice, realising that my personal morality was under the microscope. There was no right or wrong answer. I had to decide what was going to bring me the most happiness. I decided to honour my word and take the first offer.

I remember telling my father of my decision. His response was: 'I am so proud that you have done this. If I have taught my children nothing else but integrity, then I have taught them the most important thing.' I realised that my individual morality had given me something that no amount of money could buy – my father's respect.

Universal Morality

Universal morality is a moral code presumed to bring happiness to other people. It can be enormously tempting to follow the actions and moral code of someone who seems to have achieved their desires and is happy. It is easy to assume that they know how to live. They do – but their own life! It is absurd to think that they have the key to creating happiness in yours. They have created ideas and actions consistent with their own unique needs, desires and expectations and not by the standards created by others. That is what you need to do also. You are a unique individual with your own emotions, hopes, fears, aptitudes, desires, values, and weak points. The following example will highlight the highly individual ways in which we evaluate happiness.

Example

When I first emigrated to Australia, I remember having a conversation with a young woman in Sydney. At the time, both of us had been living there for seven months and she was due to return to her home country against her will, due to visa restrictions. Before leaving, she became highly agitated, saying that the past seven months had been the best experience of freedom and expansion she had ever had in her life. She was distressed about leaving and returning to a country which she considered compromised her personal values of freedom and choice. She said, 'Australia is such a fantastic place – I don't know anyone who comes here and doesn't say it's the best place on earth!'

I remember being bewildered by the statement since, at the time, I could not totally relate to her positive feelings. For me, coming to Sydney was undoubtedly a rewarding experience but at that time it was also tainted with feelings of homesickness and alienation. I remember thinking, 'I will never again ask people what they think of Australia or anywhere else for that matter.'

Australia doesn't actually exist outside the experience and subjective reality of the observer. True, there are some cultural attributes we can pinpoint but these are equally confusing, as not all individuals born within the boundary called Australia demonstrate them. Our experience of any place is a function of the uniqueness of ourselves and the circumstances in which we find ourselves at the time. To collude with the myth that there is some universal place of experience called 'Australia' is limiting. You might as well say, 'Isn't being alive good?' since this would allow for more freedom in trying to pinpoint something shared about the human condition.

Exercise 29

Think of something you do in your life in accordance with some universal moral code. It may be related to relationships, treatment of elders, or giving to the poor when you can't afford it, or something else. Write down any inconsistencies between what you believe your morality should bring you and what it does. Then write down the justifications you create for this state of affairs.

If you live by others' rules and it doesn't make you happy then you invariably suffer guilt and frustration and try to make your emotions conform to your expectations.

There are many times when living according to others' rules does not bring us happiness. Consider the justifications people make for this state of affairs:

- Upholding Christian virtues is meant to bring me peace – any anxiety I feel is because God is testing me.
- It is only right that I should forego all individual pleasure and put my children first – everyone knows that ultimately it will be worth it.

- Everyone knows that you have to forego pleasure on earth to get your reward in heaven.
- It is a normal part of any long-term relationship to go through bouts of unhappiness – if I hang in there, I will be happy in the end.

The 19th century existential philosopher, Kierkegaard, makes an interesting point about adopting the moral dictates of others. He takes the example of marriage and how sanctions were imposed on those who left their partners and sought divorce. Moral condemnation was poured on the perpetrator. In his book Either/ Or he said of marriage:

> *...it is not surprising that the attempt should be made in so many ways to bolster it up with moral supports. When a man seeks separation from his wife, the cry is at once raised that he is depraved, a scoundrel, etc. How silly, and what an indirect attack upon marriage! If marriage has reality, then he is sufficiently punished by forfeiting this happiness; if it has no reality, it is absurd to abuse him because he is wiser than the rest. When a man grows tired of his money and throws it out of the window, we do not call him a scoundrel; for either money has reality, and so he is sufficiently punished by depriving himself of it, or it has none, and then he is, of course, a wise man.*[2]

Even though our 21st century attitudes towards divorce are somewhat different, the essence of Kierkegaard's words highlights an important point about adopting the moral dictates of others. This principle can be applied to other actions allegedly grounded in some outside authority. The benefits of being moral are the rewards we reap for behaving in certain ways. If we forego these benefits, then surely we have suffered enough by being denied the rewards of being moral in the first place. No doubt there is some other moral principle which would deny this!

It is very seductive when you meet someone whose ideas do make sense to you, and very tempting to adopt ALL their ways. As with the Certainty Myth, there is no absolute certainty in the outcomes of the choices we make. Do not replicate the actions of others but learn from their ways of being to make more informed choices about your life. Universal morality is a code of conduct which will presumably bring happiness to everyone who chooses it – sadly this is not possible!

Absolute Morality

This is a morality where someone is expected to relinquish their happiness for some higher good. It is different from Individual and Universal morality. The simple definition of each of these is as follows:

- Individual morality is a self-directed code of conduct which you use to bring about personal happiness.
- Universal morality consists of dictates from someone else which, if adopted, will supposedly bring about personal happiness.
- Absolute morality comes from some authority outside of the individual, i.e. the perception that there is someone or somewhere more important than the individual.

Absolute morality dictates that the individual should be moral regardless of the consequences to themselves. In other words; doing what is right is better than one's own happiness. If you don't adhere to these principles you are pilloried as selfish, self-centred, hedonistic or ruthless by adherents to this belief.

People believe that a certain moral code is appropriate to protect the moral fibre of society. But what is society? It is a group of people with very different needs and desires and all of them have very different ideas concerning how they should live. If the individual has to give up their own happiness, what is the purpose of society in the first place?

Exercise 30

Reflect on your own life and outline any Absolute morality by which you live. This may be a religious, spiritual or societal belief. Write down what this moral code is, how it influences your life and what you believe to be the consequences of living by it.

If God, for example, said we should do something a certain way, who is to say what he/she meant? Whatever the source of what you believe to be absolute morality, you are relying on another authority to make you happy. If you believe in some holy book, remember that many interpretations exist of what was originally meant. Ultimately, you will become the authority by making a choice of whether or not to believe its contents. You have the choice to choose the morality by which you want to live, even if you cite someone else (whom you yourself have chosen), as the authority for your actions.

Remember, the only thing you can't choose is NOT to choose!

So whatever morality you choose to live by, you must judge its usefulness by its consequences. However, other people seem to take delight in advising you of the consequences of your actions. They make claims like:

- You will not go to heaven.
- You are a bad example to young people and a threat to the moral fibre of society.
- Your selfishness will catch up with you in the end.
- If you behave like that, you will end up a lonely person.

Again, you must decide whether these consequences will eventuate and whether or not they are important to you.

Absolute morality fails because:

- Even if you choose to believe there is a higher authority, you are the authority who chooses what it is and what it is telling you to do.
- You will have to consider the consequences, even if you try to fix it so you do not, so it is important to deliberately recognise the consequences and decide which ones are important to you.

Overall, no one can actually decide what is moral. Whatever you choose to attribute your choices to, you are living by an individual morality. The question is: 'Are you acting deliberately and meaningfully to make it the morality you want to live by to make you happy, or are you passively accepting the ideas of others?' Kierkegaard's earlier quote is relevant here:

> *People hardly ever make use of the freedom which they have, for example, freedom of thought; instead they demand freedom of speech as a compensation.*[24]

Remember, there is no objective right or wrong. But there is right or wrong in your own life:

- Right is what brings you happiness.
- Wrong is what brings you unhappiness.

The same rule applies to good and bad. It is hard for people to accept this and I can hear some of you saying, 'How selfish. What about killing people? Surely that is wrong!' I believe it is wrong in that anyone who kills someone has to experience the consequences of their actions and, in this case, this would probably be imprisonment or a lifetime of fear, guilt and remorse. For most but not all of us, this would not bring happiness and can therefore be considered wrong.

There are, of course, varying levels of what people consider good and bad, or right and wrong. For instance, saying no to a marriage proposal may cause the other person pain. However, it doesn't mean that we have to change our minds and marry them. In this respect, the marriage rejection may be considered a necessary pain. If we deliberately lead a person on with the intention of hurting them, that is creating unnecessary pain, and may be considered wrong.

Another example may be that of veganism. While the pain inflicted on animals is often hidden behind closed doors, ethical vegans make a conscious decision to abstain from animal products, in order to live in accordance with their Individual morality — the belief that hurting animals is wrong, whether witnessed in person or not.

However, is it wrong in some absolute sense? This is a bigger philosophical debate which is outside the remit of this book. However, perhaps the existential writer Sartre can help us out here.

The Existential Perspective

The premise on which Sartre's philosophy is based is that Existence precedes Essence. For him, there is no God nor human nature and thus no absolute morality. In his novel *Nausea*, he uses the example of the manufacture of a paper knife to explain this principle. The knife designer has a plan in mind before he creates the knife. Thus the Essence of the knife existed before it came into existence. In terms of human beings, if God knew what he was creating, then our essence would precede our existence and the concept of human nature would be a valid one. For Sartre, this is not the case, and he says, '...the essence of man precedes that historic existence, which we confront in experience.'[25]

This philosophy has been criticised on moral grounds, saying that it is pessimistic and ignores responsibility to others. Sartre counters this argument by saying, 'I am thus responsible for myself and for all men, and I am creating a certain image of man as I would have him to be.'[26]

Sartre says that the absence of an absolute authority brings feelings of anguish, abandonment and despair.

- **Anguish**: in that our individual actions influence humanity. The enormity of the responsibility causes anguish since there is no objective proof of the rightness of our choices.
- **Abandonment**: since if God does not exist, '...there disappears with Him, all possibility of finding values in an intelligible heaven.'[27] Since there is no objective right or wrong or human nature, then each of us must bear responsibility for all our actions.
- **Despair**: arises out of knowing there is nothing beyond ourselves. He says, 'It merely means that we limit ourselves to a reliance upon that which is within our walls, or within the sum of the probabilities which render our action feasible.'[28] Thus when we die, we have no assurance that our ideals will continue. 'In reality, things will be such as men have decided they shall be.'[29]

Sartre has been criticised on many fronts for his pessimistic view of the human condition. You may read him and reject his ideas. You, as the authority in your own life, can choose whether his ideas are of value to you and whether you want to adopt them in your life. The guiding principle upon which you decide whether this is right, is whether it brings you happiness and assists you in meeting your long-term aims.

In reflecting on your own morality you will come across people who appear to be rejecting the idea of a universal or absolute morality. They appear to act in ways which, to many people, are contentious and selfish. However, it may be that they are still indirectly influenced by those moral codes since they spend so much time and effort rejecting them!

Iris Murdoch talks of this as 'Cynical Frivolity'[30] - the reaction of those who are still under the sway of the morality which they deny. This means that they are people who deliberately seek ways to disbelieve the official line and act like a rebellious cynic. However, the mere fact that they *feel* they have to spend time and effort rejecting the given morality, indirectly highlights that they believe the rule to be real and absolute. Otherwise, why would they spend time trying to deny it? Murdoch suggests that instead, we pick up the lantern and go and look for the truth — your own truth!

The Morality Myth holds that you must obey a moral code created by someone else. If you act in a way to satisfy someone else's view of what is right, then it won't lead you to happiness and will trap you in commitments which will make you unhappy. It is a myth that decrees:

- You must give money to the poor because it is fair.
- You must be nice to your in-laws because they gave you money once.
- You must look after your aged parents because they gave you life.
- You mustn't buy cigarettes for people because you are encouraging them to ruin their health.
- You must send your children to church because it is good for their moral upbringing.

People delight in telling you how to live your life. Why do they tell you to live morally? Before we look at this, consider where this happens in your life.

Adhering to Others' Expectations

All of us experience others telling us how to live our lives and what is and what is not appropriate behaviour. There are many reasons for this:

- Abstinence results in later abundance.
- Foregoing pleasures now results in later rewards.
- It builds character.
- It worked for them and those were *their* reasons!

Exercise 31

Reflect on your life and outline examples of how others tell you how you should live. This may be openly expressed. For example, you may be told how you should behave as a good mother. Others may be more covert and hold unspoken cultural expectations which you only become aware of when you act contrary to them.

Telling others how to live their lives can be a powerful manipulative tool which often benefits the person using it. People have doubts about their choices, and any challenge to them is seen as creating too much conflict, so it is easier for them to influence you to change in accordance with their choices to reinforce their belief that they are right. Remember that each of us thinks differently. *A truly useful morality is to recognise that people think differently than you* – this should help you to handle those differences without bowing to the demands of others.

Your Morality

You are 100% responsible for your own life (even if someone else offers to accept the responsibility) because you are the only one who will experience the consequences of your actions. Only you can decide what is right or wrong, no matter what meaning others attach to those words. You don't have to obey the dictates you grew up with or that you hear around you. Everything can be challenged, and should be, to determine its relevance to you and what you want. As you examine the ideas of others, some will be useful and some not. Some may even be harmful. Carefully reappraise any moral framework that has been guiding your actions. The following example indicates how careful examination can reveal different motivations and reasons.

Exercise 32

Look back at the last exercise. Consider both the overt and covert examples you provided and outline the consequences of you believing the claims and expectations of others regarding your actions. What has been the real cost for colluding with the Morality Myth?

Example

In many cultures, enormous criticism is poured on individuals who choose not to have children. The possibility of being labelled self-centred is often sufficient to influence people's decision of whether or not to have children. Let us examine this more closely. The argument they give is:

- If you only have yourself to consider, you will become selfish and lonely.
- People who don't have children have no commitments to anyone.

- People who don't have children become intolerant of other people's needs.

The list goes on. However, perhaps the argument could be turned around. Maybe people who have children are actually more selfish because they had children to:

- Give them the joy of becoming a parent.
- Give them a sense of belonging to a family.
- Give meaning to their life.
- Look after them in their old age.
- Reduce the conflict brought about by others telling them they were selfish.
- Manage the anxiety of wanting something different from those around them.

If you look at it this way, having children can be seen as a selfish act carried out by some people because they want to be parents and have their needs met. It has little to do with the children's rights but chosen because *they* wanted to have children because they believed it would bring *them* happiness.

In the same way, many actions hailed as 'unselfish' may also have an underlying selfish intention. There is nothing wrong with this – we just need to appreciate that all our actions stem from a basically selfish intention – to make us happy. This is okay, and something which I believe should become the guiding moral principle in our lives, for it ultimately means we will be who we want to be and others can make the most informed decisions about their own happiness in relation to us.

As you examine the morals by which you live, ask yourself:

- Have these moral codes been developed by society to restrain individuals or are they there to make my life better?
- Am I just accepting a morality that was given to me by someone or have I chosen it out of a personal knowledge about myself and what I want?
- Are the rewards and punishments vague and intangible or will they specifically lead me to being happy or unhappy?
- Did I create them because I have a reason or is it because someone somewhere thinks it is right?
- Is the morality a current fad or is it tailored to meet my style? (An example here would be the current thinking of political correctness in all business dealings.)
- Is the morality aimed at me or against my interests or does it act for me and come from my own values and expectations?

All answers come from you. Remember that when someone expresses or writes down an idea, they go on thinking and changing long after they have spoken or written about it. The original idea was based on what the person saw and believed at the time – they may think differently now in the light of subsequent experience and knowledge gained. If the creator of the idea can change their views, then surely it would be wise for you to avoid blindly accepting the changing ideas of others? You are the ruler of your life. Personal morality is something that allows you to consider the consequences of your actions. It will lead you to do those things which bring you happiness and avoid potentially troublesome situations.

As with all ways of being that challenge the behaviour and ideas perpetuated by groups of people, you will be criticised. When others criticise you, say:

> *I am who I am – the person who will live with the consequences of what I do. No one will experience the consequences of my actions other than me. If they think they are experiencing some consequences in relation to me, it is the consequences of their own actions.*

Breaking Your Own and Others' Morality Myth

The Morality Myth is that your behaviour and actions should be in accordance with a moral code set down by others. There are three main types of morality – Universal, Absolute and Individual. However, all morality is individual since you are the one who will ultimately choose the code by which you live your life. Even if you subscribe to a code dictated by others, ultimately it will be you who will choose it.

How can you avoid the Morality Myth ruling your life and point it out in others?

- Develop a general rule to help you make decisions to avoid disasters and focus you on long-term important desires and goals.
- Develop an individual moral code which constitutes a generalised long-term attitude.
- Question universal and absolute morality, remembering that you are the only one who can judge the standards by which you live your unique life.
- Opt for freedom of thought rather than freedom of speech. The former requires you taking direct action and the latter requires you to change others.

- Do not replicate the actions of others but learn from them in order to make more informed choices about your life.
- Judge the usefulness of your own moral code by its consequences and ensure that those consequences are important to you.

Chapter 8

The Dishonesty Myth

It is preferable to be discreet, modest, or embroider the truth in our interactions with others rather than be ourselves.

Self and Identity

Numerous theories exist regarding the development of self and identity and the circumstances under which individuals fail to develop a secure sense of themselves. Miller[31] suggests that the developing child intuitively conforms to what is required to be accepted in order to guarantee them a measure of existential security. This continues throughout life with narcissistically disturbed individuals becoming attuned to others' needs and seeking relationships that require them to meet others needs to the detriment of their own.

Miller argues that the aetiology (cause or origin) of such narcissistic disturbance is found in the infant's early emotional adaptation when their needs for respect, echoing, understanding, sympathy and mirroring weren't fulfilled.[32] This has serious consequences. Firstly, it is impossible for the child to consciously experience certain feelings of its own (e.g. envy, anger, loneliness, anxiety) either in childhood or adulthood and so they become repressed. Secondly, accommodation to parental needs often (but not always) leads to the 'as-if personality.' This is rather like the False Self described by Winnicott.[33]

Miller argues that such adaptation is so complete that the individual is unaware of this and unable to differentiate it from their true self. Thirdly, in not experiencing their own emotions, the child cannot rely on them and experience themselves as a separate self. The child is thus dependent on the parents and later in life on loved ones, groups and others, and especially in their children who they can control by responding only to their acceptable False Self. All of these suggest that the developing individual must, in some way, distort their needs and emotions to be acceptable to others.

The notion of Sedimented Beliefs[34] is the existential counterpart of the notion of the False Self, although many existential writers criticise the assumption that part of ourselves conforms to external demands when a 'true self' somehow remains hidden.

It is always immediately apparent that little acts of dishonesty serve to erode our freedom. Many of the white lies we tell appear trivial but, in the long term, they create tremendous restrictions in our lives. For example, imagine you want to do something but if a certain person knows, this would cause problems. So you tell a lie to cover it up. One day you find yourself with her and another person and the matter comes up. You feel you have to repeat or confirm the previous lie. However, the other person doesn't understand the inconsistency between what you are saying now and what you said to him earlier. Thus, you have to invent an explanation to satisfy both of them. Now, whenever you are with each of these people, you have to remember the separate stories you told them to keep the original lie from being exposed. The more people that are involved, the more complicated this becomes.

Imagine the amount of effort that goes into maintaining this farce. Valuable energy is expended that could be used to bring about your happiness and well-being. Look at the price you pay to avoid revealing your actions to someone. If you admit to the second person that you lied to the first, your honesty will always be questioned in the future. Whatever way you handle it, you pay for the dishonesty. However, you may disagree that being discreet or modest represents dishonesty. For you, there may be many benefits in being dishonest.

Exercise 33

Write down the benefits you believe come from being modest, discreet or directly dishonest. Give examples of when you have lied and the benefits that have arisen out of them.

You may have cited many examples of the benefits of dishonesty. For example,

- It provides a short-cut to meeting your needs, such as someone who steals something rather than obtaining it by honest means.
- It avoids conflict, since honesty may not bring you the rewards you want.
- It enables you to influence others in the way you desire.
- It avoids embarrassment or humiliation.
- It enables you to maintain previous lies.

Exercise 34

Write down the costs of your dishonesty. Provide examples of when lying incurred costs that you were or were not aware of at the time.

I believe they will each incur costs, many of which are not immediately apparent. Before we explore some of these, consider the costs of lying in your own life.

It is a myth that it is preferable to be modest or discreet – more acceptable words for dishonesty. Once you collude with the Dishonesty Myth, you limit what you can do spontaneously. You always have to be on your guard as you try to avoid doing anything that might reveal your previous acts. Consider the problems that arise out of lying.

- You use precious resources to cover up your past acts as you are always on your guard.
- You cannot be yourself and have to hide behind an image you have created for others.
- You end up being dishonest to yourself. Lying becomes automatic and, in the end, you don't remember what is true and what is a lie.
- Because of your dishonesty, you end up feeling that you don't deserve what you get, nor can you enjoy what you have because it could be taken away from you at any time.
- When others learn of your dishonesty, they can't trust you even if you haven't lied to them before. They can't accept what you say without questioning the validity of it.
- You divorce yourself from reality and talk about your life as if it were someone else's. You therefore lose touch with your own needs and expectations.

Here is an example of how the last one might work.

Example

A friend once called me about a major trauma in her life which dramatically impacted on her and her three children. She explained that her marriage was breaking up and that she was doing everything she could to preserve the family home. This meant maintaining a reasonable level of communication with the husband until a financial settlement had been agreed.

He had not yet told his parents and I was told that if I spoke to him, I knew nothing of the divorce plans.

As I rarely rang when the husband was there, this was unlikely to happen. If the issue had arisen then I would not have colluded with this distortion of reality, the reason for which you will see in later examples, one of which is set out in the next paragraph.

I rang the eldest son on the following day to discuss how he saw the situation. His mother had told me that he was terribly upset by the situation, had been physically unwell and had been unable to attend school. Because I was close to the boy, I wanted to discuss how he was handling what, for him, was a highly stressful event. The conversation began cheerfully with the child telling me about his birthday plans. The conversation was upbeat and did not refer to the stressful reality of the family breakup. After some time, I said, 'So you have a lot on your plate at the moment – with everything going on at home, it must surely impact on your other plans?' He hesitantly said, 'So you know then...?' As soon as he realised I knew about the situation, he proceeded to tell me all about the events and say how upset he was.

By colluding with the desire of the mother to 'keep things quiet,' this child was being denied his right to engage directly with his emotions and express his needs and concerns about the situation. He had appeared upbeat, maybe in an attempt to mask his real fear and pain. Once he had been given permission to discuss the situation, he was able to put a label on what he was feeling and process what was happening to him.

Lying, in this instance, is an example of the tremendous price you pay for lying or colluding with others' lies. You begin to live in a non-reality and observe your life from a distance. In this way, you throw away your freedom.

Why do people tell lies, even white lies? There are many reasons people give for telling lies. Many of these relate to being discreet or not wanting to upset other people. However in reality, this rarely happens. If you pay someone a compliment and then say to someone else that you were telling a white lie because you didn't want to hurt their feelings, how can others trust you when you pay them a compliment? Also, the original person often knows the truth anyway, and to have you deny it results in their not being able to trust you in the future. For all our actions, we have to pay a price, that is, the risk or consequence that things may not work out as we had wanted. Maybe lying is a way of avoiding paying the price or getting something without responsibility for the consequences? However, in the long term there is always a price to pay.

We are encouraged to lie in all walks of life. The Dishonesty Myth goes with the Identity Myth of being what others want us to be and acting in ways to create an image that will be acceptable to others. You only have to look at films, books and newspapers to see how people lie to get what they want, to avoid hurting others and to avoid chastisement. Consider these:

- The promises of politicians who claim to be acting for the public good.
- Clandestine lovers who have secret meeting places whilst married to other people.
- Employees who mask contempt for senior management in the fight for promotion.
- People who spend time with people they find boring in an attempt to be seen to have a good social life.
- The person who feels they must continue lying because telling the truth as a child was not always rewarded.

There are as many reasons given for lying as there are instances when we lie. However, there is always a cost to lying - you either get caught out directly as someone learns of the lie or you must live with the anxiety that, at any time, you will be found out. You always bear the weight of knowing that once another sees your dishonesty, they have no real assurance that they can trust you. More importantly, you learn not to trust yourself. Let me give you an example of a young woman for whom lying became a way of life.

Example

A client once asked me for advice as to how she could save her marriage. Her husband had discovered that she had lied about paying several household bills. Because this had become a common feature, which resulted in debts being accrued, he had given her an ultimatum – to stop lying or face the end of the marriage. She was highly distressed by the price that her lying was apparently going to cost her.

We spent some time exploring the nature and extent of her lying. It appeared that lying had become so much a feature of her life that she regularly became confused with what she believed to be the truth and what she believed to be a lie. She had lied her way through previous relationships, through jobs and lost friendships. We then explored the purpose and function of lying in her life.

She had been raised by her mother, who was English. She had never known her father, who was Asian. She had attended a school at a time and place where cultures different to those of the English were rare. 'Foreigners' were treated with suspicion and prejudice. This is where her lying had begun. She forged an identity which was more comfortable for her – to tell people she was English/Spanish. This seemed to her to be acceptable, since Spain seemed to be a glamorous holiday destination. Thus, the benefit of lying was an alleviation of her anxiety and acceptance by classmates.

In any situations where she sensed anxiety and fear, she adopted the strategy of lying since it had helped her in the past. The only problem was that lying does have a price, although it may not be paid for some time.

Lying for my client had been a useful strategy in the past. It was now becoming a burden and incurred a cost she was unwilling to pay. However, before she was able to relinquish her lying behaviour, she would have to recognise the value and purpose of it in her life. Once this value was offset by the higher price of living with the consequences, she decided she would have to change. It was only by her recognising that lying had been a useful part of her life as a child, that as an adult she could live with the consequences of her actions and protect herself. Thus she began the road of learning about herself all over again.

So what are the benefits of dispensing with the Dishonesty Myth and becoming honest? Before you decide whether relinquishing lying in your life is the right choice, you might like to consider the benefits of this new way of being.

Exercise 36

Look back to your responses in the last two exercises. Consider the benefits and costs that lying brought you. Consider your examples and outline the benefits you would have enjoyed had you not lied.

Here are some of the benefits of honesty:

- When you show you are honest, no matter what the short-term consequences, others will accept your word confidently. You will access opportunities you would not have had if they had to question what you were saying.

- You can relax and not have to think about whether what you are about to say will contradict a previous remark.
- When you are honest, you learn that you often don't know what others want to hear anyway. You may have made lots of assumptions, but by being honest, you might be projecting a more attractive image than the one you could have made up.
- Others often become more open with you. When you reveal aspects of yourself, they are able to reciprocate and feel safe in revealing hitherto hidden aspects of themselves to you.
- When you have lived honestly, you know that you deserve what you have. You won't have to fear that one day you will be discovered and all you have achieved will be destroyed.
- You will be free to share private aspects of yourself with others as you won't fear their judgement. This will also encourage them to be honest with you, since they observe that being honest means they are freed from judgement as well.

Maybe the answers to your previous exercise indicated these benefits. Maybe they gave you ideas that you had not appreciated before.

Exercise 37

Think about your life and the benefits you identified of being more honest. If you did not identify any in your previous activity, consider the above six benefits, and identify ways in which you could benefit from being honest if you changed your behaviour today. Provide examples from your life now.

The benefits that you identify will be personal. Let us now take each of the six benefits listed above and look at how they might operate in practice.

- **When you show you are honest, no matter what the short-term consequences, others will accept your word more confidently.**

  Consider a relationship between a couple. How often does one partner say to the other, 'I love you' to immediately receive the reply, 'I love you too.' These protestations may seem very reasonable and affectionate. But sometimes one of the partners may not want to reply with 'I love you too.' However, not to offer a response is greeted with the question, 'Well you do love me, don't you?' To avoid conflict, many people find it easier to automatically reply rather than express exactly how they feel at the time. Often these requests come at a time of argument or disagreement when one partner, despite the desire for reinforcement from the other, does not want to have their intentions challenged. Feeling loving may be the last thing they feel at the time and yet their whole commitment is challenged. How much better to allow others – and more importantly ourselves – to be spontaneous. Thus, when someone says 'I love you' it is because they genuinely want to tell you rather than saying what you want them to say at a specific time.

When you are honest, people will relax around you as they will not have to be on their guard, checking out everything you say.

- **You can relax and not have to think about whether what you are about to say will contradict a previous remark.**

Consider a conversation between two people who have just met socially. One person begins a conversation on a subject of which the listener is less knowledgeable. The first person briefly asks if the listener knows a particular writer they are about to discuss. Instead of the listener admitting their limited knowledge about the writer, they nod politely and give the speaker permission to continue. The speaker, with full confidence in the ability and knowledge of the listener, offers a sophisticated and witty account of the subject. The listener continues to nod politely but his smiles and laughter are matched by rising anxiety as he longs for the speaker to finish and be safely directed towards another subject before the listener's ignorance is recognised.

On many occasions, this strategy might be valuable and allow the listener to move smoothly from one social encounter to another without the anxiety of admitting his limited knowledge on what, after all, he believes 'people in such social situations should know about.' However, there are occasions when the listener will become more anxious as the speaker, reinforced by the listener's attentiveness and presumed knowledge on a subject so few people have a grasp of, attempts a deeper and more sophisticated discussion of the subject. The listener now faces the additional possibility of being found foolish as he tries to change the subject.

All this could have been avoided if the listener admitted his shortcomings and allowed the speaker to moderate their rendition or teach him something important about an interesting subject. In this example, the cost of dishonesty is the anxiety and presumed shame of being discovered as ignorant and a liar. The benefit of honesty is the opportunity to learn about an interesting subject on which the speaker is only too glad to offer a simpler explanation. The politics of the situation are apparent whereby knowledge constitutes power and the relative power positions of the individuals.

- **When you are honest, you learn that you often don't know what others wanted to hear anyway.**

  Consider a conversation between two friends regarding one's vulnerability regarding a career change. Person 1 may perceive their friend as confident and never questioning their own ability. However, this may not be the case. Because Person 1 believes it, it becomes their reality and Person 2 is unable to express their fear and self-doubt since it may be criticised or doubted. Person's 1's greatest desire might be that Person 2 show themselves to be vulnerable and less than perfect.

- **Other people often become more open with you. When you reveal aspects of yourself, they are able to reciprocate and feel safe in revealing hitherto hidden aspects of themselves, to you.**

  In the previous example, if Person 2 had the confidence to reveal what they considered to be a less attractive aspect of themselves, there could have been numerous benefits. The relationship might have become a more intimate and accepting one rather than projections of images of what each believed to be desirable. By being honest, we often give permission to others to be honest too.

- **When you have lived honestly, you know that you deserve what you have. You won't have to fear that one day you will be discovered and all you have achieved will be destroyed.**

  I remember a work colleague of mine who lied about finishing his university degree. Every time he applied for a job, he said he had obtained an Economics degree, which had given him a sound background of education at graduate level. In fact, he had only completed one year of the four-year program. Years later, he paid the cost of this lie. Every time he applied for a job he lived in fear that his tutors might be contacted for references. He also feared meeting clients and peers who had been at the university at that time. The price of his lying was the fear of being discovered.

- **You will be free to share private aspects of yourself with others as you won't fear their judgement. This will also encourage them to be honest with you, since they observe that being honest means they are freed from judgement as well.**

  In the previous example of the two friends, Person 2's honesty might have resulted in them receiving much-needed support from Person 1 and feeling more valued as their friend opened up to them and asked for help.

Colluding with Other People's Deception is also Lying

Many people say that they lie to protect others' feelings. Despite being an admirable claim, this is not the case. It is usually to avoid the person disliking them. It is rarely about making the person feel better about themselves – it is about them feeling better about the person giving the compliment or agreeing with them.

Imagine someone asks you for advice about an aspect of her life. She feels that her failed marriage is due to her husband's bad behaviour. We don't do anyone any favours by colluding with their Dishonesty Myth that holds that their marriage was bad because the husband was unreasonable. Whilst he may have been unreasonable, he could not have been unreasonable without her permission.

To allegedly make your friend 'feel better' by denigrating the husband, doesn't do anything to make her life better. To question her role in allowing herself to be treated in this way might be a more honest stance. Lying in this respect never works. Once the person learns to accept that she had a role to play in her poor marriage, she will no longer have any respect for your views.

Exercise 38

Think of an occasion in your life when you lied to 'protect' another person's feelings. What was the purpose of this and what were the benefits and disadvantages to you, them and others of this dishonesty? What would the benefits have been if you had been honest and how would you have given this advice to avoid alienating them?

Do not be afraid to tell people the truth. How can people learn and reflect on their own behaviour if we deceive them further? It is worth remembering how powerful it can be to maintain our integrity as highlighted in Nelson Mandela's inaugural address as President of South Africa, 1994, quoted in Chapter 3.

By lying, you also damage your credibility with other people. Say someone asks you what you think of someone else, and you say that you don't like them but have not told the person because you didn't want to hurt their feelings. Look at the cost of this statement. When you say something nice about the person you are with now, they won't believe you. People look to see how you treat other people in order to judge how you will treat them!

Many people say that in order to 'smooth' interactions in everyday life, it is essential to be discreet and tell white lies; to bluntly tell the truth in every situation would result in conflict and argument. This is not so. There is an alternative to being blunt.

Example

I remember a conversation with a girlfriend on my fortieth birthday. Here is the dialogue:

Clare: I have really started to develop lines around my eyes over the past year. What do you think?

Friend: Yes, I have noticed that you have developed lines. However, they are actually rather attractive. Who wants to be 40 and yet look as if they have no life experience or wisdom?

This may seem a simple example, but it was a more honest interaction than I had with several other friends. Other friends had colluded with what they thought I would like to hear. They said, 'Oh don't be silly – it's nothing that an early night won't sort out.' This wasn't really what I wanted to hear. It wasn't really an issue about my lines. It was an issue about growing older and wanting to be considered attractive and acceptable to myself. By engaging with my real concerns and not diverting them by focusing on cosmetic issues, I was able to accept them as an inevitable but attractive aspect of maturity.

> Many people go along with others' demands to 'turn a blind eye' to certain information which arises out of others' lies. The previous example of the boy whose parents were undergoing a divorce highlighted how colluding with others' demands results in us denying the reality of our own and others' lives.

We don't have to hurt others' feelings by being blunt. The above example shows how recognising my real concerns and identifying the positive aspect, my friend was able to be honest and at the same time supportive. It is often better to concentrate on an aspect of a person's behaviour rather than on them in totality. For example, rather than saying, 'I don't like you,' you could more realistically say, 'There are many things I like about you but I don't like what you are doing in this instance.' This recognises the broader context in which the issue at hand is only a small part. Honesty makes it easier to deal with what has caused the problem. It may be that the problem between people is too little truth rather than too much!

Recognise that you are sacrificing your reputation and reducing your alternatives if you lie as a supposed favour to someone else. Any problem they have in facing the truth is their problem. If you collude with them, it becomes your problem! It is not your duty to protect people from themselves nor can you do anything about their feelings!

There are many occasions when you have to decide whether colluding with someone else's behaviour is compromising your honesty. A common situation is when you see someone being treated badly by someone else. If the people in question are not important to you, you may be able to walk away and not allow it to affect you. However, what if the people or one party is important to you?

Imagine a situation in which your close girlfriend is subjected to a degree of emotional bullying that you find unacceptable. You witness this on several occasions in the form of put-downs, criticism and belittling of your friend. It causes you to become angry and resentful. You may implore your friend to address this behaviour and make a stand with her partner, whom you consider to be a bully. How can you maintain your integrity and honesty in this situation? To ignore it when it is happening in your presence would certainly be colluding with the behaviour. However, there are other, more subtle ways in which you may deal with this.

Imagine you see the couple together and witness the derogatory way in which her partner speaks to your friend. This is not an acceptable minor conflict between the two which you just happen to witness. It is an insidious, deliberate attempt by him to attack her very person and demean her in front of others. You may decide, 'Well, this is her choice – I want to see her and if that involves him being there, well I will just put up with it.' You may feel that it is none of your business, since what happens between two people is their business. You have been honest enough by imploring her to find someone better. However, are you being completely honest with yourself and with them? To continue to witness the bullying, are you not, in some way, saying that the behaviour is acceptable? I think a better stance would be to challenge their behaviour directly and act on your convictions. Perhaps something like this:

> *I am very uncomfortable with what I consider to be bullying of my friend. I appreciate that you both choose to be together and that she cannot be bullied without her permission. However, it is not sufficient for me to express that this is unacceptable. To stay in your presence is to collude with this behaviour and, implicitly, accept it. I am therefore removing myself from your presence as an indication that I do not*

> *agree with what is happening here. From now on, you will know that I act on what I say. You will be able to trust me, since what you see of me will be exactly what I stand for. If I stay you might interpret this as secretly accepting the situation despite verbally expressing my displeasure.*

You may, of course continue to see your friend separately, having expressed your position. You may also decide not to say anything – that is your choice. However, you may decide that her lack of self-respect and values are so far removed from yours that you no longer have enough in common to constitute a friendship. She may also make this decision.

Exercise 39

Think of an example in your life where you have colluded with someone else's unacceptable behaviour. It may be unacceptable behaviour towards yourself or which you witness in relation to someone you know. Make a list of the benefits that would accrue by you not colluding with their unacceptable behaviour.

There are a number of benefits of not colluding with others' unacceptable behaviour.

- You or your friend will know that you have your own or her best interests at heart and are there to support each other.
- You will respect yourself and will demonstrate through your own self-respect how your friend can learn to respect herself.
- Other people will know that you are a person of your word and willing to put into action what you say.

- Other people will trust you as a result of your actions.
- You will be able to trust yourself and avoid living with the anxiety of having your values compromised.
- The bully in this situation will have an example of someone gaining respect without the need to inflict power over another.

Being 100% Honest in All Your Interactions

You can only be sure of your honesty if you are 100% honest with everyone. We all create stories to lie to ourselves. Consider some of the following situations:

- If you lie on certain occasions, how can a friend be sure that you are not lying now?
- If you say you are lying to protect another's feelings, how does your friend know you are not trying to protect their feelings now?
- You may claim that you only lie if absolutely necessary. How does the person in front of you know that now is the time that it isn't absolutely necessary?
- You may say that you don't lie to friends. How does your friend know when they have left the close circle called 'your friends'?
- Perhaps you'd never consider stealing from someone but would feel comfortable lying to an anonymous job-holder in a company. What are the consequences of this? If you can lie to someone you don't know or value, and whom you believe will not be personally affected by your dishonesty, imagine how much more you could lie to keep something that was important to you, such as your relationship with me?

If you want to prove your honesty, be honest with yourself. People will be able to trust you since you will have demonstrated that you will be honest, even when it is uncomfortable for you to do so.

Exercise 40

Look at the above five examples of the values around dishonesty. Do any of these look familiar and fit with your current personal morality? Can you give examples for any of them and describe what you perceive as the cost and benefits of being dishonest?

Often we lie without realising it to put our best foot forward and to say what we think we ought to say. For example, you may have developed a way of relating to one of your parents that is much better than before. However, you may find yourself lying to them, not because it is how you want to be represented but because you are unwilling to shake the already fragile foundations of the relationship. You have to ask yourself how important it is for you to compromise who you are in this situation.

Reflect on your day. Sometimes you will realise that you have lied without even realising it. This lying may be subtle and masqueraded as 'smoothing' social interactions. However, you are compromising yourself whenever you lie and will pay the consequences at some time in the future.

Example

Have you ever noticed how some people's behaviour changes in the presence of their partner? Imagine someone you work with of the opposite sex, with whom you have a jokey, flirty relationship. Neither of you necessarily has a sexual interest in the other, but share a way of relating which is childlike and spontaneous. Now imagine that you meet their partner at a social function or after work. Notice how your colleague's behaviour might change. You may not even recognise them! The spontaneous, fun person has become serious and distant from you – presumably to avoid any confrontation with their partner, who might challenge them as to their relationship with you. They are, of course, living the Identity Myth – that there is a 'right' way to be in relation to 'others' outside of the intimate relationship. They simply do not feel safe enough to be open and spontaneous with others outside of their role.

I know a couple who have been together for nearly twenty years. When I am in their company, I am acutely aware of their individuality yet also of the strong bond which exists between them.

The woman in the partnership has kept contact with a couple of previous partners with whom she shared a special relationship, and a couple of times a year she meets them for dinner and is open with her existing partner about this. He jokingly says to me, 'You know, most women have a hobby and my partner's hobby is seeing her ex-boyfriends!'

On speaking to her separately, she highlights the degree of trust and respect they have for each other. The fact that they both accept that there are people in their lives who are important to them validates each of them, and is what contributed to them becoming the people they are today. He isn't trying to deny aspects of her life that made her the special person he wants to be with by limiting who she interacts with.

To maintain this trust is what makes her happy – to violate it and risk losing someone who accepts her for who she needs to be is the cost she would pay for operating outside the boundaries of their relationship.

To be around this couple is electric – the trust, spontaneity, integrity and fun is contagious. It is in sharp contrast to many other relationships I encounter, where each partner denies ever having had important relationships with other people. Who wants to be with someone who has never loved anyone else?

I would not want to be with someone who wanted to deny the things that had contributed to who they wanted to be with – me. To deny the reality of previous relationships or behaviours is to deny the unique me that exists today. I challenge you to think about this.

Maybe you are wondering how you should deal with past lies which have a reality now. How do you come clean and drop the pretence? It will certainly be challenging to tell other people that you have not been totally honest. However, you will find out who your true friends are. Often people relax more around you because they suddenly see you as human and vulnerable and this reflects on the very feelings that inhibit their own honesty. It may surprise you also that once you tell people a truth that you have been hiding, they reveal that they knew you were lying all along! What stopped them challenging you was the dishonesty in their own lives! They continued with the lie themselves to avoid paying the cost – maybe of losing your friendship!

A great sense of freedom will come when you drop the pretence. You will be able to forget about the contradictions and complications you had to keep track of. I have already said that the only way to demonstrate your honesty is to be 100% honest. The most ineffective way to demonstrate your honesty is to say, 'To be honest with you...' This existential position indicates that what you have said before was dishonest or that you are expecting others not to believe you. It plants the question in their mind of whether what you are just about to say is bona fide.

By being honest you will attract the type of people you want to be with rather than people you don't. You will become a more attractive person, putting all your energies into who you want to be rather than who you are trying to closely resemble – the person who is like everyone else is trying to be. Fashion is a good example of this. It also happens with all other aspects of our behaviour.

People fear the exposure of being 100% honest in their interactions. Remember that people are too busy worrying about their own inadequacies to worry about yours! You will find a number of reactions. The first may be acceptance and a relief that they also can drop the pretence with you and be who they want to be. Others will use your honesty to bolster their own sense of importance and ideal of perfection. They will be unable to be honest themselves and will ultimately pay the price for this.

The Importance of Integrity

Honesty is displaying yourself to others as you really are. You cannot be truthful about something you don't know. Therefore you need to develop a relationship with yourself so that you know more about who you are and can understand and accept the multitude of things that constitute the unique you. Only when you know who you are can you honestly represent yourself to others.

An individual who doesn't know themselves:

- Cannot speak with authority about themselves.
- Cannot make promises because they don't know themselves well enough to forecast their future emotions and actions.
- Cannot express authoritative opinions because they don't know what they believe.
- Cannot be honest with themselves.

Honesty involves the integrity of knowing yourself and saying what you want, with authority. People say 'I believe' or 'I want' but often don't have a close relationship with the one who has created those sentences. People will judge you by your actions, and how you treat others will indicate to them how much they can trust the relationship you have with them.

Example

I remember a time when I used to expend my energies on trying to influence the impression I made on others. If I felt I had been misrepresented, I would rush to provide the necessary information to change the negative impression I thought had been made. I felt that in some way it was important to present a consistent impression to others, and enormous anxiety resulted if I was unable to influence this process. I claimed that 'this is not how I am normally,' as if an upset at a social occasion, for example, could destroy who I was in their eyes.

It then occurred to me that these variations to the 'norm' were often seen positively. I appeared as more complex and interesting – someone who was unafraid to portray aspects of themselves that previously had not come to light. It also gave others permission to do the same and allowed me to develop a more concrete sense of myself – someone who was not a fixed object but one who is constantly being created through relationships with others. It was only by developing a surer sense of who I am that this was possible.

Breaking Your Own and Others' Dishonesty Myth

The Dishonesty Myth is that dissembling is preferable to being discreet or modest and that it's OK to embroider the truth in our interactions with others. This chapter has shown that this is not the case. The benefits of honesty can be enormous; dishonesty is a costly and expensive exercise. The effort of preventing others from knowing things about you can be costly and draining. To hide yourself through dishonesty is highly self-destructive and a habit you can easily get into. It is also reinforced through every aspect of our culture and socialisation. It is particularly difficult to break out of dishonesty if you have learnt that it is valuable, if only in the short term.

Example

A couple I know were in the process of divorcing. The husband told the wife that during their fifteen-year marriage he had never loved her, despite telling her to the contrary throughout the relationship. He even lied at the marriage ceremony but interpreted this as mere wedding nerves. He now felt that his marriage was a sham, however, he said that he loved his children and would continue to support and see them after the breakup.

It is interesting how this person, who has professed to not being honest about his own utterances and behaviour, can expect others to believe him now. To tell his children that he loves them whilst admitting his deceit is to ignore the very real effect his dishonesty will have on them. He tells his wife that he said he loved her even though at the time this was not true. Maybe the children will also think that what he is saying to them now is a lie, in light of the fact that he has been able to live a lie of which he was very consciously aware. To no longer have feelings for someone is very different to claiming to have them in the knowledge that this is not the case.

> Remember that honesty and its converse – dishonesty – have consequences, and that people can only trust you if you have integrity and honesty in relation to yourself and all others.

The Dishonesty Myth is a form of the Identity Myth. When you lie, you are giving in to the temptation that you will appear more acceptable, more attractive, more successful, more desirable and will obtain what you want if you appear to be different from what you are. However, the cost is enormous. Learn to trust yourself and your own identity. You will miss more if you don't. You can face each day without the clutter and baggage needed to cover up past deceptions.

How can you avoid the Dishonesty Myth ruling your life and point it out in others?

- Acknowledge that dishonesty is costly, and valuable resources are wasted in colluding with your dishonest acts.
- Foster 100% honesty so that others don't question your word and you do not have to cover up your lies.
- Examine all areas of your life and eradicate even the white lies.
- Identify the purpose of lying in your life and work out a cost and benefit analysis. You will be surprised to find that lying always incurs a greater cost than honesty.
- Reflect on the increased trust, individual awareness and relief you will experience as a result of being who you truly are.
- Avoid colluding with others' lies which masquerade as not hurting others' feelings.

- Enjoy the enhanced credibility that comes from being honest in all your actions.
- Recognise that being honest gives others permission to be themselves as well as giving you a surer sense of who you are.
- Drop the pretence of being what you think others want you to be and embark on a journey of getting to know the author of your life.

Chapter 9

The Myth That You Can't Change

You are fixed and certain in your being and earlier choices negate future change.

Process versus Essence

The existential notion of freedom and choice implies that we must choose our existence. Existential theorists remind us of our tendency to deny our freedom, instead, blaming others for our predicament and limited options. The concepts of Bad Faith and Inauthenticity indicate the means we use to deny responsibility for our lives.

Accepting responsibility for our lives is challenging but offers the opportunity to live with passion and purpose rather than duty and obligation. Psychotherapy offers an opportunity to more deeply examine our lives and address issues that inhibit our sense of well-being and freedom.

Existential Psychotherapy invites individuals to experience themselves in relation to another and to experiment with different ways of being. It encourages the individual to find meaning and significance in their life and engage with the enormity of their life choices.

Existential Psychotherapy distinguishes between self as 'process' and self as 'essence,' whereby the self is seen as '...a centre of gravity which is altered as we enter into contact with the world.'[35] Psychotherapeutic change thus comes from the 'in-between,' at the point of our involvement with the world.

By the time you reach this chapter you may have mixed feelings and reactions. You may be denying the possibility of radical change, believing that it would only be possible were you able to shed your debts, your work and your commitments. You may be saying, 'If only I could win five million dollars I could make all the changes I want.'

To impose these conditions on your life is to shed responsibility for your life. In many ways, it is a myth that you can't change. Even if you don't knowingly make changes in your life, changes will inevitably occur, requiring modifications to be made. Why wait for pressures or other people's plans to initiate change in your life? You have unique abilities, talents, dreams and ideals. The biggest issue is getting in touch with how you want to use them. You can increase your income, get out of debt, reduce your working hours or have more satisfying relationships. However, they just don't arrive one day. You are the author of your life and if you want to change in a meaningful and informed manner, there is always a way. As said before though, there is always a price. Are *you* prepared to pay the price?

Example

On several occasions I have asked people, 'What would you do if you won five million dollars?' The answers in terms of achieving goals and realising dreams are as varied as the people answering. Here are some typical responses.

- I would immediately have more time
- I would give up my job
- I wouldn't feel so tired all the time because I would buy in lots of help
- I would travel and see the world
- I would do full-time environmental and animal activism
- I could do anything I wanted to do – wow!

For me, five million dollars wouldn't enable me to buy anything I want that I couldn't buy now. This is not because I have already acquired such wealth, altruism or hold particular socialist values, but comes from a real feeling that anything I want is attainable now. I would still choose to spend time with other animal rights campaigners and have conversations about how to create a kinder world. I wouldn't change the partner I live with now or the direction of my life. Whilst budgeting might play a different role in my life, I have never been a person whose increase in income immediately matches an increase in spending. With five million dollars I might decide to live by the sea, or would I? If I really wanted to do that I could do it now as I work a lot from home. However nice a place by the sea might be, I would still want that same group of like-minded people around me to enjoy the experience.

Ask yourself the question, 'What would I do if I won five million dollars?' Your answer may provide you with valuable insight into the dreams and desires you have which you only uncover in the belief that they are not attainable because you don't have five million dollars!

What can you learn from this example? It is a challenge to encourage you to think very carefully about what you *really* want and whether you are avoiding hearing it because you believe it is only attainable if there were a miracle. However, that is a Myth – you *can* make changes that contribute to your happiness – in the short and long term. But first you must get in touch with what it is that you want. This chapter will give you an opportunity to do this, how to get there and the price that is entailed in realising your dreams.

Preparing for Change

When you decide what you want in the long term, it is often easy to compromise and withstand the obligations you consider are necessary to achieve your goals. As time goes on, these obligations and commitments become onerous and problems exist long after the long-term goal has been achieved. This happens in many areas in our lives. Consider marriage. You may have desired a loving relationship with someone special and marriage may have represented the means to attain it. However, within that contract other duties and expectations might have arisen which seem unrelated to your long-term goal of a loving relationship. This might be unacceptable to you, but you choose to compromise despite considerable discomfort.

The same goes for the long-term goal of a high-status job. You may have started out with a desire for the status of a responsible, high-profile job and you may have worked very hard to achieve it. However, now you have attained this goal, you are sharply aware of the duties and obligations that represent compromise in how you lead your life now. Even in small things, you will find that routines and schedules you considered useful earlier continue without you ever appraising their usefulness and contribution to your current goals.

It is crucial that you regularly check to look at your assumptions about your life. Assumptions are those things that you hold to be true without even questioning them. Reappraise your activities and look at your short- and long-term goals to see how much relevance they still have to your happiness. A useful way to do this is to look at what you do with the 168 hours of each week and consider how meaningfully you are spending your time.

Exercise 41

Take a large sheet of paper and write down exactly how you spend your 168 hours per week. A standard format is provided in the Appendix. Write down all your activities as they are now, without any judgement. Next, rate each activity as:

Enjoyable, Unenjoyable or Indifferent

Rate as enjoyable those activities that you choose to do and from which you derive some happiness. Do not rate activities as enjoyable because you don't know what to do instead. Do not impose judgements on what should be enjoyable. You may go to the gym regularly but find it more of a chore than relaxation.

Think about your work. Sub-divide your work activities and label different tasks accordingly. Activities labelled as unenjoyable are those where you have to ask, 'Why am I doing this? Is it necessary? This is a chore. I feel obligated.'

Then label activities that you are indifferent about. These may include brushing your teeth or walking the dog.

Positive or Negative

Next rate your activities as positive or negative. The positive ones are those you choose in order to make you happy. An example may be going for a walk when you could have chosen to do something else. The negative ones are those you do to avoid unhappiness. For example, visiting the family to avoid conflict with your partner would fall into this category.

Active or Reactive

Activities labelled as active are those which you initiate or choose to do. An example might be enrolling for a night class. However, it would be reactive if you enrolled to please your boss.

Are you going along with things because they are considered to be part and parcel of what you want or wanted at some time? Are you allowing others to choose for you? If you always allow others to choose for you, you will never find happiness, since what makes them happy will be different for you.

Label as reactive all those activities that someone else wants you to do. You may visit your parents regularly to keep them happy when you dread the conflict and fights that ensue.

By labelling your activities, a picture should develop of how much of your life you are actively choosing to bring about your happiness.

Reactive activities

Let us consider reactive activities for a moment. Reactive activities are also those you do to preserve a relationship, even if it is unimportant to you. Ask if the time spent doing this activity is worth it. People say that compromise is necessary, but if you are with the right people – those with whom you share important values – self-sacrifice and compromise are not really necessary! Look for relationships where you don't need to tolerate unpleasant things to maintain the relationship.

Reflect for a moment on your labels and decide why you are doing those activities. Ask yourself if they contribute to you achieving your long-term goals or are they encumbrances that you haven't considered or which you feel are necessary to achieve what you want. Are they enjoyable? Are some of them the result of earlier commitments or past mistakes? Now let's consider how productive they are in bringing about your happiness.

Exercise 42

Look at each of your activities and label them with one of the following:

Enjoyment – those activities which bring you happiness right now, e.g. watching films, cooking, tennis.

Past mistakes – those activities which arise out of something you did in the past. This may be a financial commitment to a cause you no longer support; financial settlements on a previous marriage or a work obligation continued because your friend got you the job and you would feel guilty if you left.

These two labels build on the earlier stages and highlight how much choice you are exercising in your life now. The next activity goes further, and focuses you on the future and how productive your activities are in contributing to your short- and long-term goals.

Exercise 43

Now label your activities as:

Productive in the short term – this applies to anything you do which makes you happy now or will do shortly. It may be aspects of your work which generate money that you can spend enjoyably right away. It applies to plans and energy spent on arranging holidays or home renovation that gives you pleasure.

Productive in the long term – activities which you believe will bring you happiness in the future apply here. You may be training to work in a new area that you believe you will enjoy. You may be working hard for a retirement home, and this is something you eagerly anticipate. The criteria you apply here is whether it contributes to your future happiness.

Unproductive – some activities appear to be done with no real hope of bringing you enjoyment. This might apply to committee meetings you attend for some voluntary cause you no longer support. It may be hours watching NetFlix to avoid thinking about your life rather than for enjoyment. It may be more radical and be a relationship that you hoped would bring you happiness but only brings conflict.

You might find that different aspects of the same activity are labelled differently. That is why it is important to work through the activities hour by hour. You will see from the last two activities that the labels apply to different times in your life:

- Past – past mistakes and commitments
- Present – those that you enjoy
- Future – how productive they are in the short and long term

This exercise may be causing you some alarm as you reflect on the hours you spend on activities that simply do not make you happy. Applying labels is a way of highlighting how much you enjoy in your life, how much is duty and how much contributes to bringing about your happiness in the short and long term. It focuses you on seeing how frequently you do things to please others or because you never have time to appraise their value.

Ask yourself now, 'How much of my 168 hours per week is making me happy?' Try not to justify everything you do now as contributing to a long-term goal. This can be a cop-out since the answer, 'I put up with a boring job with an aggressive boss because one day I will have earnt enough to live in luxury' is a life sentence! You don't have to suffer now to reap benefits later. In a sense, the future is a myth too, since it represents hope which is experienced in the here and now.

Labels help you to simplify your life and encourage you to change so that life is not just obligation. You may be thinking that to change so much is too difficult. Certain changes will bring about anxiety, conflict, loss and negative reactions from others. However, what if you don't change? Now you are more aware of how much you enjoy in your life, not changing means spending every day knowing that you are unhappy with little opportunity of it changing.

Change involves living with anxiety. Ironically, to not change is also living with anxiety. That is the human condition. How much better to live meaningfully in anxiety where you have better odds for happiness! So let's start with small steps.

Exercise 44

Find some time every day to do something out of choice. Take some time every day to reappraise your actions now to see how they contribute to your long-term goals.

You may find it hard to do something out of choice every day. It may have been a long time since you really engaged with your needs. You may also say, 'I am always choosing what to do and where to go!' This may be the case, but look again. Ask yourself, 'Would I choose this if I had complete freedom?' You may find that the reply is not always 'yes.' Life is not complicated – you make it so. Other people don't make your life difficult – you allow them to cause you difficulty. Even if you don't actively seek out conflict with your boss, to continue with it is a collusion for which you must take responsibility. Where you find yourself now is a result of choices you have made along the way. You have chosen to be where you are today and you can choose not to be!

...ivities, values and assumptions that exist now and no longer fit your life can be changed. This refers to bad relationships, jobs, obligations and commitments. It doesn't mean you can relinquish your responsibilities, it means you must calculate the cost of change and pay the price for it. Change begins with the decision and then action.

How Do I Change?

In order to change your life from what it is now to what you believe would make you happy, you must first work out what your ideal life would look like. You can then use this as the criterion against which all your activities can be judged, and those which don't contribute to your ideal life can be eliminated. The following activities enable you to take this ideal journey. By the end of it, only you can choose whether you want to take action to bring it to fruition.

Exercise 45

Imagine you are starting with a completely blank slate. You are on your own and free of all obligations and commitments. Write down exactly what you would do with your life if you knew you could not fail. The two paragraphs following this exercise might be helpful in doing this, so refer to them first.

Be as creative as you want to be in choosing what you would do. Remember that this is your ideal. Don't be put off by thinking that it would be impossible to achieve. At this stage you can live your dream on paper. Remember that you can't change others but you can imagine what it would be like to have people in your life you spent time with because you really wanted to. Of course you may include people and things in your ideal life that you already have. Don't include anything or anyone only because you can't imagine what it would be like without them.

Write as much detail as you can, and when you have finished, close your eyes and imagine yourself living that life. Carry this image around with you for the next few weeks and at regular times reflect on it. After a while a core image will probably emerge. It will represent the focus around which your ideal life is centred. Make a note of this – it will help you with the next step.

Exercise 46

Take your list of labelled activities prepared in Exercises 41-43 and cross out anything that doesn't appear in your ideal life. Reflect on what is left and what proportion the remainder is of your current life. This will enable you to get more in touch with the reality of your life now.

You will now need to consider what to do to achieve your dream life. What actions will you need to take and how much will it cost you? If you want to train as a doctor, you will need to study, become qualified to get into medical school, find time to devote to your effort and pay for your studies whilst supporting yourself.

Exercise 47

Consider what will be entailed in achieving your dream and note this in detail, including:

- Requirements
- Time
- Resources
- Knowledge
- Money
- Personal Costs
- Emotional support

It is very tempting to modify your dream because it seems impossible, given your present circumstances. Try to avoid this, since you will never be happy unless you have a clear picture of what you want.

The next stage is to look at your current assets and liabilities since these have implications for how and when you realise your dreams.

Exercise 48

Outline in detail your current assets and liabilities. List savings, capital, money owed to you, belongings and insurances under Assets. Next, list debts, hire purchase, credit card balances, mortgages, loans and regular financial outgoings. List these under Liabilities. Work out the total of both your assets and liabilities.

If your financial assets are more than your liabilities, this represents what you have to make your new life. If your financial liabilities are greater than your assets, don't be tempted to ignore your dream until you have paid off some debts. Don't procrastinate until you have enough money, since it is your current actions that have contributed to where you are now. There is no assurance that continuing as you are won't offer you more of the same rather than a path to your new life.

In reflecting on your liabilities, it may become apparent that they indicate certain social and moral responsibilities. Changing your life doesn't mean relinquishing your responsibilities. Meaningful living means facing up squarely to your responsibilities and paying the price for them. A person might say, for example, 'I just couldn't leave my disabled wife because it is morally wrong.' Actually, they could leave their disabled wife – the only thing that stops them is the choice that the cost of leaving in terms of the personal, social and moral obligation, is too great for them. Choosing to live authentically and meaningfully means embracing the fact that you have choice and freedom. But our freedom exists within certain givens.

For example, if you have no use of your legs, you will not become a runner. However, within these givens, you have enormous choice – even if only attitudinally.

Example

Seb Alex is an example of a man who changed his life dramatically. Born in Beirut, Lebanon and trained at the prestigious University of Paris, he gained a Bachelor Degree in Architecture and a Masters Degree in Sustainable Architecture and Environmental Design. His expertise led to him being sought out by leading companies and he became the Coordinator of International Projects of a large architecture and engineering company, where he managed large teams on complex projects.

Seb had always had a keen interest in social justice activism and was inspired by people like Malcolm X and Martin Luther King. Life changed suddenly for him after watching Gary Yourofsky's famous speech at Georgia Tech University, opening his eyes to the scale of animal suffering in multiple industries, and compelling him to look further. He watched a documentary called Behind The Mask and then Earthlings; the life-changing documentary outlining the animal abuse industries in the United States. These insights further fuelled a desire within him to speak out and help end the animals' suffering. In his words, 'The more I looked into this, the more I realised I had to get active.'

Despite a promising career ahead of him, Seb left corporate life to live in a way more closely aligned with his values, including an end to animal suffering and its resultant effects on people and the environment. He now lives a minimalist lifestyle, educating people worldwide of the imperative of veganism and non-speciesism.

Seb is an example of someone for whom radical change was the key to a new life. Seb's philosophy is that aligning your life with your values and becoming who you need to be always pays dividends. The risk he took in walking away from his career and becoming a full-time animal rights activist has been worthwhile. His astonishingly large following is testimony to the positive effect he has on others, who feel inspired and equipped to go out into the world and make it a better place.

Making your Dream a Reality

The following paragraphs identify ways in which you can make your dream a reality. It is worth rehearsing this in your mind before you take action but remember that to achieve your ideal life, action is required.

I recall watching a video of Elisabeth Kubler-Ross interviewing an old man who was near to death. Elisabeth was a Swiss psychiatrist and author who revolutionised the thinking around helping those dying to depart with dignity and respect. The words of the dying man struck home to me when he said, 'I made a good living but I never learnt how to live.' Don't wait until your death is on the doorstep before you take action.

Look at your assets and if any of them are not on your dream list, get rid of them. Liquidate all those superfluous assets which may include your car, your house and your belongings. At the same time, eliminate all those activities that don't contribute to your ideal life. Use the cash to pay off your liabilities. You may find at the end that you are left with no assets. However, you will have lost nothing – you will have gained freedom. Which is better? Assets and obligations with no time to change your lot or freedom with no encumbrances to realising your dream?

Terminate all relationships with friends, contracts, courses or engagements that don't make you happy. I can hear you saying that you need to keep working to provide a roof over your head and food on the table – for yourself and maybe others. This is okay. It takes time for your dream to materialise. A note of caution here: many people continue with a job, for example, as a means of income until they train for something else. However, they become so comfortable with the status quo that this temporary measure becomes a rut. Don't allow a means to an end to result in you leading a life of quiet desperation.

If you think you have to keep your current job to finance your move towards your dream, work out the minimum input required to meet your needs.

If you want to maintain a relationship with your parents, does it really require you to visit them twice a week? Which is preferable? A son or daughter who visits willingly and who enjoys the visit, or one who grudgingly resents their parents because they feel guilty if they don't visit frequently? You may feel they put pressure on you to visit regularly. However, this might reflect part of *their* ideal – to have a son or daughter who wants nothing more in the world than to visit them. If you don't feel the same, however many times you visit, you will not contribute to meeting their needs, since your actions will not match their desires. They are not missing anything by your visiting less regularly. In fact, they only serve to gain if you visit willingly and freely. Think about this! Work out what is right for you and keep your ideal life in mind at all times.

Exercise 49

Look at the changes you wish to make. Write down exactly any resistance you expect, and from whom, and identify ways in which you could explain your actions to them.

When you begin to make changes in your life, expect to encounter resistance in the form of anger, resentment and blame. People will say you are selfish and that you are ignoring your responsibilities. Remember that a large part of this is because you are not behaving in accordance with *their* notion of happiness. It has little to do with *your* happiness.

You will recall that the Dishonesty Myth suggests that it is preferable not to be totally honest. I suggest that you be totally honest, since the price you pay for embroidering the truth accrues interest, especially when you are anticipating further change. Tell people that you are reappraising your life and that you are being selfish – taking responsibility for the direction of your life and examining the options for your happiness. Be honest that this is an evolving process and that you cannot answer all their questions at this time. Live with the anxiety that others may put pressure on you, withdraw their friendship or sever ties with you completely.

Ask yourself, 'Are these the people I want in my life? If they are not prepared to allow me time to reflect on my life choices, do I want them in my life anyway?' It is not always easy, but is the cost of maintaining the status quo so great that you must pay the price with your whole life?

Starting from Scratch

It is a very seductive proposition to stay as you are once you realise the costs involved in making change, despite the costs of staying put being much higher. You may decide it is simply too hard. You may feel that the resistance from others is too great and that life is unfair to have placed you in this predicament. Remember, you can change anything. Work out the price you will have to pay to achieve your ideal life. Decide how much you are willing to pay for it or for certain aspects of it. Decide at what point it is not worth making the change.

Example

Andrew came to me for coaching since he wanted to further develop his career as a professional leadership coach. To date, Andrew's career had been extensive and he had worked initially as a chartered accountant for seven years and a chartered surveyor for four years. However, he had always found these areas of work highly stressful and had experienced two heart attacks, one by the age of thirty-five and one by forty-two. Andrew had always been interested in working in the area of professional coaching and yet, to date, his working life had left little room to develop his skills further. He had tried to move into coaching but financial commitments and the pressure of others' demands kept him focused, first on accountancy and then on marketing. He believed that these lines of work provided a level of income and security that matched his lifestyle and commitments.

Andrew had been unhappy for some time but after his second heart attack he began to question his life choices and make some difficult decisions regarding his future direction. He resigned from his senior marketing role and focused his time and financial resources on learning all he could about coaching. This process involved him using substantial amounts of his money as he studied and travelled extensively to seminars and workshops.

After four years of study and no income, pressure began to weigh heavily on Andrew and his family. Despite Andrew being happier than he had ever been, the financial demands of his lifestyle and family resulted in him entering serious debt. With the memory of two heart attacks behind him, he was reluctant to take paid work unless it matched his ideal of providing the most effective coaching service.

The day came when Andrew found himself in his house, rapidly losing its furniture since the bailiffs were taking his remaining belongings away to recover his debts. One of the bailiffs said to him, 'You look like a reasonable chap; why can't you get work?' He told the bailiff about his previous heart attacks and his desire to develop a professional coaching business. The bailiff said that his brother worked in this area and made a quick call to introduce Andrew's services. That phone call resulted in Andrew being given a two-year contract as a coach and he was able to rebuild his life.

Andrew's remarkable story highlights that it is possible to make change in your life despite the most difficult of circumstance, if only you are willing to pay the price. Andrew's 'attack of the heart' encouraged him to examine his choices and the price to be paid for changing or maintaining the status quo.

Don't allow others' reactions, punishments or threats to throw you off course. Take your commitments and responsibilities seriously and try to satisfy them as soon as possible by incurring the costs. Revisit the chapter on the Commitment Myth. Remind yourself of these principles:

- Take responsibility for your choices and don't blame other people, society or social norms for not exercising them.
- Recognise that you can change almost everything in your life as long as you are prepared to pay the price involved in this transaction.
- Identify things in your life that you would prefer not to do now but continue with because of previous investment. Remember that the only way to gain the equivalence of resources wasted so far is to use your time, money and efforts now exactly how you want to.

- Don't try to change the world. Embrace the freedom you have now and see the additional benefit of acting as an example and catalyst for change in others.

The only real commitments that cannot be taken seriously are lifetime promises. Think about this for a moment. I can hear you saying 'But that is ridiculous!' The Commitment Myth says that it is impossible to change certain things in our lives once we have committed to them. This is *not* the case. To expect yourself to make choices at one stage in your life with no opportunity for change later means that whatever arises out of that earlier decision has to be tolerated. To live like this is to live inauthentically and to choose to live with less than is possible. Commitments do have prices too, but to give up your whole life to maintain a commitment is unreasonable.

Imagine Yourself Paying the Price

Go over in your mind all the possible reactions in yourself and others that might arise when you take action to change. Imagine yourself paying the price, responding to anger and accusations; experience the pain felt by others and yourself, and living with the ambivalence which arises out of the anxiety of change. Work through all the possible scenarios, including the worst ones until this exercise is no longer painful. For example, telling your children that you love them very dearly and them begging you not to leave; the withdrawal of friends, the anger of a loved one or blame and recriminations of others affected by your decisions. Look at contingencies and what could go wrong so that you are emotionally prepared for any eventuality.

Exercise 50

You may find it difficult to go through all the details in your mind since, initially, this may be a very frightening experience. To help yourself, write down all the reactions – in yourself and others – that could *possibly* happen. When you have written this several times, go over it in your head until you can do so without pain.

Pay the price and don't opt for a life of quiet desperation rather than facing a short, sharp, sudden pain. You cannot avoid the price owed for your choices but if you don't make it now, you may have to pay it every day you have left. This time, however, the price has increased because of the knowledge you now have of the ideal life you have abandoned.

It is very easy to put the needs of others before your own but, as described in the Selfishness Myth, this is like passing a gift to another where no-one ends up realising the gift. If you died today, people around you would carry on without you. The benefit of choosing the life you want to live is that you mirror to others the importance of living authentically, having examined what it is you want and knowingly living every day.

You may fear that you have thrown away a very important gift, such as family life. However, the highly stereotypical illusion of family harmony is a Myth. It is an idealised, internal image that we all hold up and work towards. But that's all it is. Family life does have the potential for support, love, growth and safety. It also has the potential to harbour anger, guilt, shame and violence. If you are not happy, who is benefiting from this collective arrangement?

You may believe that it takes a long time to build deep friendships. Now is the time to test the foundations of your friendships. Would you prefer to be with people, not knowing whether they would support your quest for happiness? Alternatively, you can challenge their friendship, knowing that you have lost nothing if they reject you once you reveal you want to be true to yourself.

Recognise what it is that you want from your relationships and decide what you are getting and at what price. If the equation doesn't balance, decide how you might be able to get a better deal somewhere else.

Often what we fear we are losing is something that we desire but don't have, such as an ideal family life, or a loving relationship. We haven't lost anything from such a situation but the gain is in leaving the sadness and frustration of it not being realised.

When you make changes, expect to feel withdrawal symptoms since we do make strong attachments to others. If you are prepared for this, you will survive in the knowledge that you are being true to yourself. You will have identified the necessary resources – internal and external – to help you survive the aftermath. You also won't be patronising people, believing that they can't live without you.

I strongly believe that if you do what is right for yourself, then ultimately, it will be right for others. Therefore, recognise what you have to do. Anticipate paying the price demanded in advance and expect strong emotional reactions in yourself and others. Ask yourself, 'If I knew I was going to die in six months' time, what would I do with my remaining time?' Once you realise that you would not have time to go around arranging everything to satisfy others – and some would be disappointed that they could not spend precious time with you – then what would you do? You would recognise this reality and focus on what you needed to do to make the best of your precious time.

Well, you *are* going to die. You don't know when it will be. You may have less than six months or one hour. Don't wait to live until you know you are going to die.

The film *Life as a House* portrayed Kevin Kline who, learning that he had cancer and four months to live, quickly refocused his life and became more honest in his interactions and expectations of others. Don't leave it until circumstances, health, fate or old age pressurises you to change – embrace your life now and make the changes you, and ultimately others, will benefit from.

Breaking Your Own and Others' Myth that You Can't Change

The Myth that You Can't Change says that you are fixed and certain in your being and that earlier choices negate any possibility of change in the future. This is simply not true. Earlier commitments and obligations can be relinquished and you *can* carve out the life you want to live.

What can you do to facilitate change in your life, when the enormity of the change seems too great to face? How can you point it out to others?

- Recognise that you are the author of your life and that you can make informed and meaningful choices.
- Accept that embracing your freedom will bring you anxiety but that the rewards will be enormous.
- Examine the assumptions by which you live your life and change them if they no longer work for you.
- Reappraise your daily life and consider how your actions contribute to your short- and long-term goals.
- Identify how you spend your time now and focus on things that are enjoyable, positive and catalysts in bringing about your happiness.
- Look for ways to eliminate those activities that are unenjoyable, negative or reactive, for they will only negate your path to freedom and happiness.

- Consider the balance between your short-term activities and their contribution to your long-term happiness. Do not compromise your time now to achieve some promise of happiness in the future.
- Begin change now by doing something out of choice every day. Be ruthless as to whether this is your choice or whether it is chosen from a narrow range of choices you believe are available and socially acceptable.
- Appreciate that the rewards of having people in your life who want you to be happy are priceless.
- Plan your dream life now and imagine paying the cost of getting it.

Chapter 10

Next Steps – Helping Others Change

By the time you reach this chapter, you will realise how many myths operate in your own life, many of which you were probably not even aware of. This will provide you with greater insight into what is going on in other people's lives when we ask them to change – it's not black and white or as simple as just choosing between different options. The choices we give people are embedded within socially and culturally shared assumptions which are also related to their identity and sense of belonging. When you ask someone to change, it throws them into anxiety that not only may they stand out from groups or a connection with consensual reality they feel safe in, but into anxiety within themselves that suddenly their worldview (and thus their identity) is about to change.

Having examined your own life and the underpinning myths, you're probably asking yourself some questions about changes you'd like to make to your life now. You'll also be more understanding when others become aware of the myths and start asking questions. You also understand why it is so hard for people to change, especially when other people with whom they share their worlds haven't yet had those insights. For example, someone who becomes aware of the hidden costs in animal agriculture and how their consumer choices fund this, may decide it is wrong and become vegan. However, their friends and family resist this change, interpreting it as non-acceptance of shared traditions and meanings rather than ethics about animal exploitation.

I imagine that you picked this book up asking why people won't change and how you can influence them to break through their own myths. For those passionate about causes beyond themselves, communication skills alone rarely offer sufficient understanding of why people cling to choices, when many of them have such negative consequences on themselves and others. This is not a book about communication techniques or how to trick someone into changing. It is about getting people to come to terms with the conscious and unconscious choices they are making or not making, and how this trance of assuming there is 'no choice' in certain circumstances is shaped by myths. We already have freedom now to be who we want to be. Freedom isn't 'out there' – it is right within us and it takes us and them some time to fully grasp this. I believe that real freedom is about freedom of thought and meaningfully choosing the lives we want to live, in-spite of the anxiety that often arises from feeling we have been outcast from the norm. Embracing freedom comes with a cost and those who break free from the trance are marginalised, ridiculed and resisted. Usually it is not until some time has passed that these people are eventually seen as the trail-blazers or renegades, whose message is now considered obvious.

Change can be uncomfortable and sometimes excruciating and, for many, seemingly impossible. Each person has a different capacity to embrace change. This book invites people to examine their choices to date and ask whether, in light of new information, those choices still serve them, their family, society, and the world at large.

In the modern world, these Myths are so interwoven in our thinking that we cease to question their existence or roles in our lives, yet they are major determinants of how we live our lives. Myths provide a context within which to understand how hard it is to change, because existential anxiety arises as a person's sense of who they are in the world is fundamentally challenged.

In this section, we look at how you can identify and respond to myths operating in other people's lives. We'll examine how people's motivation to change or not change is underpinned by their pain and pleasure motivators. Then, having also grasped that we can't change anyone except, in some cases, by brute force, we'll identify practical ways in which we can influence them to change. There are things you can do as an individual to increase your influence in inviting them to embrace change, as well as becoming part of the collective change through embracing part of a consciousness-raising alternative to many of the challenges we are faced with globally.

The Impetus for Change

People who work in sales know that people are influenced to buy things when it meets their needs. Broadly speaking, they act to move towards pleasure or move away from pain – physical and/ or emotional. Myths tend to operate in ways to avoid pain; the pain of feeling different, alienated, not part of the group, or anxious because you are left with 100% responsibility of doing something that is different to what the masses do. Myths also hoodwink people into believing there are set ways to be happy, successful, safe and fulfilled. You only have to look around you to see the vast majority of people doing the same things, even if those choices cause discomfort now for the promise of the reward later. For example, doing a job you dislike to earn more money than doing something more fulfilling for the reward of financial safety, reputation or later freedom. For many there is safety in numbers, so they would rather live with the anxiety of not being true to themselves rather than the discomfort of being an outsider.

If you want people to change for something beyond themselves, you must understand how avoidance of pain and pursuit of pleasure work. For example, if a parent learns how their current lifestyle contributes to serious environmental destruction, their pain is likely to increase as they consider the consequences for their children. They might be open to changing but need to be convinced of the facts so they can weigh up the advantages of changing versus living as they are. Some people, when shown cruelty in animal agriculture, are deeply disturbed and immediately empathic towards the victims, so stop eating them. Others may be momentarily distressed but divert their attention to how animal-based foods injure their health. This, together with the promise of greater energy and health might be a greater 'pleasure' influence on them changing than the 'pain' of thinking about animal cruelty. In other words, the strength of people's pain and pleasure motivators vary enormously.

Increase Their Pleasure or Decrease Their Pain Motivators

When a person doesn't change on something we know would benefit them and a wider cause, we often simplify why they do this. For instance, if a daughter becomes vegan for ethical reasons and shares with her mother what happens in animal agriculture, she may believe that her mother's refusal to change is because she is selfish and more concerned with her own taste-buds. However, the mother may observe her daughter overcome massive health challenges that she would like to experience too. In other words, she wants the positive pleasure of improved health by adopting a plant-based diet. However, when she thinks about changing, her pain also increases as she believes she will no longer be able to cook traditional cultural dishes and would face criticism from her husband, who thinks vegans are extremists. If the daughter provides her mother with plant-based recipes of traditional Italian food, she reduces her mother's anxiety and belief that she has to change everything. This is known as getting 'early wins' and when a person makes changes on small things, they are likely to embrace bigger changes in time.

Another example would be that in some countries that have only relatively recently been able to access western luxuries, people may associate eating meat and drinking milk as sign of wealth and westernisation. So for them, asking them to revert to a more plant-based diet would be seen as a step back, despite all the evidence that it would benefit their health. It would be more difficult to influence these people to change and relinquish a recently acquired 'pleasure.' It may take a celebrity or another influencer to provide them with even greater kudos by shifting to a plant-based diet.

You Can't Make Anyone Change

It is important to grasp that you can't change anyone — they have to decide for themselves. In certain circumstances you can impose force, but you can't remove the freedom they have in their own minds to think and believe what they want. Force is imposed by our policing and legal systems, yet people still choose to break the law. A person can choose to drive over the speed limit, rob a bank, attack another person, and there are consequences for those actions. However, they can still choose whether or not they want to do this.

As a reader interested in getting people to change, it's common to become frustrated when others won't change, even when you share the costs to themselves, others, and the environment. For example, you may want someone to stop buying single-use plastic, to recycle at home, resist 5G in their town, stop eating animals, shop from outlets that don't exploit workers in the third world, and so on. Facts alone will not be sufficient in changing their behaviour. So how can you assist them in coming to the realisation that choosing a different action, way of life, or belief will be beneficial? In other words, if we can't change anyone, what can we do to get them to choose differently?

In over thirty years of private client sessions and leading group training programs, I have never been able to make anyone change. However, what I have been able to do is show them the choices they have which to date, they have probably denied, ignored or been unable to see. When people engage with greater choices of how to live their lives, they learn to take 100% responsibility for their actions and reactions to what is around them. They become examples of what is possible and, in the process, invite others to live more authentically.

Individuals who hold a vision of a better world, must start to lead by example. When sufficient number of people with a similar vision find each other, they usually organise themselves to collectively speak out more powerfully. An individual who holds part of that collective vision and who takes 100% responsibility for their life, can't blame others for society's predicament, such as the government or other groups of authority. Instead of looking outside of themselves for someone to 'do something' they realise that perhaps, they may be 'the one they've been waiting for.'

As the reader, the best you can do is prepare yourself for this time, so when you are needed to join or develop a group or Movement yourself, you will be ready. Becoming an invitation for change is what you can do now to prepare for that day.

Becoming an Invitation for Change

From the moment we are born, we are subtly and directly influenced by our family and community to adopt certain acceptable or desirable behaviour. Through our family, schooling, culture, and society, this behaviour is bounded within social and cultural myths and unquestioned expectations of what's appropriate. Despite our individual differences, we still broadly conform to those myths, with many of us never questioning that they exist. Other people act as powerful role models of whom we aspire to be. Consider the power of celebrities in getting people to change their consumer habits. Their followers only do this because they believe that doing what their chosen celebrity does will increase their pleasure, for instance, they will be cool, more attractive, successful, or fit in with the 'in-crowd.' They also believe it will decrease their pain, such as feeling like a loser, unsuccessful, odd, un-cool. Using this social principle that people look to others for what to do, you can become an invitation which others can follow.

Example

Imagine you have been suffering from a number of a chronic health challenges like diabetes, hypertension or eczema. You adopt a whole-food, plant-based diet and you dramatically decrease your symptoms and in some cases, totally recover. You would be overjoyed and want to share your solution with others close to you, so they too can benefit. One person, when presented with the facts and seeing your success might change right away, or at least try your diet. Another person however, will say, 'It's ok for you. That wouldn't work for me as I have a different blood-type, I'm older, I have been diagnosed with "XYZ" condition,' or other excuses. Your frustration and judgement of them would be likely to increase dramatically, especially when they won't even try it or watch a video or read an article with the facts. On the face of it, it's ridiculous but their resistance, when seen through the language of myths, is more understandable. They are relinquishing responsibility for their capacity to choose (and instead are holding steadfast to what their doctor or diagnosis says) and are denying they have a choice to change.

Choose Your Own Battles

Our families are often the hardest to influence to change. This is because there are power issues within families with many parents refusing to believe that their grown-up children know better than them, and because it disrupts the familial myths of co-identity, predictability, and tradition. Also, family often say and do things to other family members they would never say to others and have no problem in dismissing your advice outright. If this happens, continue to live your life in line with your values without insisting they change. They are more likely to listen to people outside of the family who, with the same message, will influence their actions. Instead, become the best version of yourself and as other people see the results they desire, they are more likely to ask for your advice. Don't give people the excuse of not entertaining change because they might shoot you; the messenger, and dismiss you as preachy. Instead of telling people what to do, share your story and results without judgement and invite them through using collaborative communication skills (see below) to choose differently and experience the results. Remember, people also need to come to their own conclusions and believe they are choosing things themselves, even when the irony is that so many are blind to the myths that limit those choices.

Put Your Own Oxygen Mask on First

If you are angry about social injustices and people who won't change because of what you see as their own ignorance, closed-mindedness, or selfishness, this will soon deplete you. Instead, identify what you are feeling and ask yourself, 'What can I be or do to become the best invitation for others to change?' In order to do that you must put your own oxygen mask on first. You must work through your own distress of knowing what many others don't, as well as the frustration at blatant attempts by individuals and organisations to keep the truth from people because of their own self-serving interests. It's important to become resourced to be best the voice for your cause and you have to move through what may be great depths of anguish and misanthropy to envision a more conscious world. As you will see later in this chapter, this not only makes your life enjoyable but is essential to influence change at a global level.

Here are 3 things you can focus on to increase your influence as an instrument of change:

- Managing Your Emotional State
- Managing Your Physical Well-being
- Improving Your Communication

1. Managing Your Emotional State

Neuroscience research has revealed a phenomenon called The Contagion Effect. This is where one person picks up the emotional state of another person without any exchange of verbal or non-verbal communication. The blood flow in the brain corresponds to the areas for experiencing (or influencing) positive or negative emotions. Blood flows to the back of the brain to the 'fight or flight' area when negative emotions are experienced, and to the frontal cortex at the front of the brain when a person feels more positive. If one person is seemingly open-minded, confident and calm on the outside but seething with anger and frustration inside, the other person will pick up on this. If they are highly self-aware they might realise that it is the other person but if not, they will tend to just feel negative. Whatever the content of the conversation, it will be seen in a negative light if we are negative underneath. So when talking about your cause, it's important to ensure your internal state is open-minded and non-judgmental, so blood flows to the front of your brain and you facilitate them doing the same through the Contagion Effect. If not, you run the risk of minimising the potential for the other person to grasp what you are saying and fully consider its implications.

It's normal and understandable to feel powerful emotions like anger, rage, despair, depression and hopelessness when you look around at the state of the world. By learning to be calm and focused on the inside, you will increase the effectiveness of your communication and avoid being influenced by their negativity. This requires you to put in place routines and practices of physical and emotional self-care. This, together with improving your communication, will increase the potential of others listening to your message and changing. Here are some tips to ensure your emotional wellbeing:

Develop a Positive Mindset

Your thoughts, feelings and experiences are intimately linked. When you feel something negative, stress hormones adrenaline and cortisol are released and you feel negative sensations in your body and you're likely to say something like, 'I feel awful, angry or disgusted.' This triggers more thoughts, which release more stress hormones and this interaction results in labelling the emotion where you say, 'I am angry or defeated' (or another label). Over time, the connection between your thoughts and feelings becomes so intertwined and automatic that the body remembers and it becomes a habit. The slightest trigger or association with the initially provocative information automatically results in a negative feeling and labelling of yourself as 'angry, resentful, depressed, or other emotion.' When you see, hear, or think of something related to this topic, before you know it, you feel all the emotions as if you were experiencing the original provocative event.

The same thing happens with positive emotions. This time, happy hormones dopamine, serotonin and oxytocin are released, and you feel hope, safety and trust. In short, whatever you spend your time thinking and feeling creates your personal reality and to your change this, you must change your thoughts, feelings and actions. By deliberating focusing on positive things you start the process of change but where negative thoughts are too deeply embedded, meditation, NLP, or professional therapy can assist.

Meditation

Your mind and body do not know the difference between real and imagined events. For example, when you wake up in the middle of the night after a nightmare, your body shows all the symptoms of fear as if there were a real threat: increased heart rate, anxiety, fear and sweating. Once you realise it is only a dream, you change your mind and personal reality and yet, moments before, you felt that the threat was real. This is the premise upon which sports psychologists use visualisation and mental rehearsal to improve athlete performance.

To create a new Personal Reality of a More Conscious World, you must spend time focusing on the world you wish to create, in your thoughts, feelings and actions. I encourage you for as little as five minutes each day, to visualise and experience the positive world you want to create, as if in the present moment. These steps are a powerful way to set a clear intention and associate it with an elevated state of positive emotion. Quantum physics reveals that our imagination doesn't just create a feel-good factor, it is correlated with changing physical reality. In short: 'What you focus on, you create.'

The more you focus on the positive effects of your cause rather than the stress and anxiety of consumerism, environmental damage, animal cruelty, or the fear-mongering media, the more positive you will become. You then become part of the rising tide of social awareness of greater consciousness and bring that day closer.

People around you will notice the difference and be more likely to trust what you say because there is congruence between what you say and what you truly feel. You will avoid coming from a place of judging others, so they are more likely to listen because they feel you have their best interests at heart.

Become Your Best Ally

Many change activists are traumatised, have low self-esteem and blame themselves for not doing enough to help the cause. This self-blame can result in destructive habits and punishing yourself rather than being your own best friend. Become your best ally and through mindfulness, meditation, exercise and other self-care regimes, you will develop a sanctuary within yourself which will sustain you over the years. You will also become an example of a calm, confident, and decent person who people aspire to follow.

2. Managing Your Physical Wellbeing

Practice Good Nutrition

To remain healthy, vibrant and energised, it's important to adopt a whole-food, plant-based diet. It not only contains the essential range of nutrients for optimum health, but also facilitates healing and cell repair, slows down the ageing process, and energises the body. Many social justice advocates play scant attention to nutrition, instead focusing on the philosophy of their Causes, or ensuring no animals are harmed in the process. Avoid the highly processed plant-based diet which not only inhibits optimum health, but results in sugar cravings, irritability or moodiness, and feeds vystopia. Check out http://nutritionfacts.org and download Dr John Gregor's smartphone app, *The Daily Dozen* to ensure maximise your nutritional literacy and optimise your health.

Exercise Regularly

Find a regular exercise that you enjoy and which either provides you with solitude or opportunity to meet with others. Not only is exercise essential to build strength, stamina and flexibility, it's directly linked with mood. Depression can be lifted with regular exercise as it's linked to chemicals release in the brain. Exercise helps you sleep better and aids digestion and raises energy levels.

Relax and Have Fun

Many social justice advocates want to spend every spare bit of time they have in furthering the Cause. Only then is their anguish assuaged and they can live with the knowledge of what is going on the world that so many remain blind to. Others feel guilty that they once were financing human, animal, or environmental destruction with their consumer choices and won't allow themselves any enjoyment or ease. Remember, bringing about positive social justice change is a long road and one which you must be prepared to walk next week, next month, and in the coming years. If you burn out you won't be able to be part of the solution, so factor some relaxation and fun in your life with like-minded others as resourcing yourself to go farther and further for your Cause.

Minimise Stress

Stress is your reaction to life's external events as well as internal memories of experiences. It's your body and mind's way of telling you things are out of balance. Make a list of what causes you stress in your life see what you can take out to create more ease. Don't spend time around negative people or overcommit to things that put too much pressure on you. Learn to say 'no' and set boundaries with other people. Adopt a stress-reducing practice like yoga or other relaxation techniques so you can regularly bring yourself back to a state of calm, especially after advocating.

Educate Yourself

Commit to life-long learning about what is happening in the world so you become a well-informed individual who is able to speak with conviction and impact. Having facts and figures to hand will provide you with a level of gravitas to any discussion with others who often are quick to attack and ask you for evidence. Over time you will acquire more information and by practising having conversations about your Cause you will eagerly look forward to people asking you questions, knowing that you can back up your arguments with lots of relevant and powerful information.

Gather Support

Across all losses and stressors in life, the biggest factor in a person working through things is the extent to which they have social support. Having others with whom you can share your feelings and seek guidance goes a long way to helping us recover and make sense of life's changes. Invest in your relationships, knowing that people need your support too. Many social justice advocates only feel totally accepted by people sensitive to issues they are speaking out on, particularly when their pain is linked to what they know about what is happening. However, advocates also have lots of other concerns. Give and receive support, but ensure you jointly develop ways to navigate through the pain rather than allowing negativity and misanthropy to result.

3. Improve Your Communication

Getting people to embrace new ideas about how their behaviour impacts wider social issues can be challenging. This is because people think you are directly criticising their lifestyle and choices, and they resist that more than the reality of how their choices are negatively impacting other people, animals, and the environment. Thus, you must learn tools and techniques that enable you to have difficult conversations easily. Here are some key skills to help you:

- Challenge your own assumptions and myths about other people's intentions.
- Remain open minded and don't assume people don't care about what you are saying. Resistance is often due to self-consciousness or feeling blamed for the world's problems, rather than resisting the content of your message.
- Develop active and empathic listening skills and ask more questions, check out what other people mean and adjust your message when they don't understand.
- Active listening skills comprise:
  - Mastering the inner voice
  - Deciphering emotional meanings
  - Using non-verbal cues to indicate listening
  - Asking open and closed questions
  - Paraphrasing and seeking clarification
  - Reserving judgement during information gathering
  - Encouraging the speaker to explore new issues
  - Summarising

These skills are outlined in detail in Chapter 5 of *Communicate: How to say what needs to be said, when it needs to be said, in the way it needs to be said.*[36] To access a free copy of this chapter entitled, 'Empathic Listening Skills: The First Rung on the Ladder' visit: https://communicate31.com/empathic

Pinpoint the related hooks or topics that interest them and use these as a way to engage their interest. Common hooks include health, physical and financial security, democracy, freedom of thought, philosophy.

Focus on moving people along what I call The Continuum of Awareness (see below) from having no interest in the implications of what you are sharing to embracing change. Speak to people where they are at, realising that most of us require repeated exposure to new ideas before we change our own beliefs. You don't have to do all the work. Realise that they may also hear about these issues from others, TV, adverts, and social media, and make a connection with different angles of your message they are interested in. Ensure that your input to their continuum of increasing awareness is the best you can offer.

Become an exquisite communicator so you influence people to change. Learn to have difficult conversations where emotions are very high, and people have different opinions and views. As someone passionate about a social cause, you may want to tell them everything you know about the issues, but this can result in resistance. It's not always what the other person is interested in hearing and forcing your own agenda won't establish rapport or allow you to explore other subjects later. Bombarding someone with details of how plastic bags are killing sea life, how coal-seam gas is causing climate destruction, or animal cruelty in factory farms, while relevant and important to share, may result in resistance if they are more concerned about their family's health than the wider social ramifications of their actions. When you have explored their interests, you can add more information to expand their understanding.

It's important to realise that you don't have to convert everyone on the spot and a useful concept to understand this, is The Continuum of Awareness.

The Continuum of Awareness

Imagine that every person you meet (including yourself) is on journey towards increased consciousness, compassion and awareness. Let's imagine it runs from 1 to 10, with 1 representing absolutely no interest in social justice causes and only interested in oneself, and 10 indicating a person wanting to hear more and likely to change their actions. Your job is to listen carefully to assess where they are on the continuum and provide information, insights, and education to move them towards increased awareness.

1. resistance ⟵⟶ 10. ready to change

You do this by identifying what is known as 'hooks': topics that literally hook the person in by providing them with something about the cause they are concerned about. For example:

- Health
- Environment
- Animal Cruelty
- Job Security
- Economics
- Social Norms
- Freedom of Thought
- Philosophy

For example, imagine someone says, 'I have enough to worry about without thinking about what state the planet will be in, in fifty years!' If you answer, 'It's not all about you – do you know how much your children will suffer if we continue to destroy the environment?!' you will make them confused or angry, because they will feel attacked. Remember they may be confused with the different arguments and certainly don't know as much as the passionate environmentalist. By acknowledging their overwhelm, you establish rapport and can move into providing information about how their non-action will have far-reaching effects for their family in the future.

By using hooks, you provide people with information to expand their thinking on an issue. If you use information that doesn't relate to their interests or current world view, you'll lose rapport and they'll resist you. You don't have to change people's consumer habits right away. Some people learn information about human, animal, and environmental destruction and change right away; others take time. Your job is to move them along the continuum so they emotionally engage with the information and come to the conclusion on their own. After all, you don't want someone to have a knee-jerk reaction to an image and say they have changed their mind, yet later revert to their old habits. You want them to change permanently. Time spent nudging them along the continuum provides greater probability that any changed attitudes, values or behaviour will be permanent.

Myths of Choice: Why People Won't Change and What You Can Do About It is about embracing the reality that you and others are already free – you only have to get in touch with that reality! Freedom is a way of being, one in which you continually examine your life choices and ensure that everything you do is chosen meaningfully. Whilst pilloried as selfish by many, this is really only a Myth perpetuated by those unwilling to live with the anxiety that meaningful living brings. By understanding this in your own life, you will be equipped to understand why other people might find it difficult to change and cling to existing frameworks. They may be fearful that change will involve losing their friends and loved ones – which may happen. It might also involve them in opening up their eyes to how their choices contribute collectively to our world.

Social movements are a collective way of breaking the Myth that we can't change or that we are we are tied to old ways that no longer serve us. Activists who collaborate with others to challenge the status quo in ways that benefit animals, people, and the planet are often seen as renegades or rebellious. However, in time, their message will be self-evident and mainstream. Your challenge is to live authentically, challenge your own and other people's myths, be bold, and have the conversations that matter. Be an example that people wish to follow.

See you on the path!

Chapter 11

Existential Philosophy and the Myths

The myths discussed in this book provide a more easily understandable way to grasp complex social and cultural influences on a person's choices and identity. They explain existential concepts that, in the original philosophical texts, are difficult to grasp. For the reader who would like to understand more about existential philosophy and its significance in a person creating meaning and identity in their life, this chapter outlines key concepts in a way that is more readily available to the layperson.

What is Existential Philosophy?

Anyone who has grappled with the concepts of existential philosophy will appreciate the difficulty of applying it to their own life. The writings of Nietzsche, Sartre, or Heidegger, whilst original and innovative, are complex and difficult to grasp. Their ideas also challenge the premise on which much of Western thinking is based. Nietzsche[37] stated that 'God is dead,' leaving us to find meaning beyond some supernatural power. Sartre suggested that 'Existence precedes Essence' and that we are free to create ourselves in any way we wish. Heidegger offered the concept of 'Dasein': We are an existent, 'thrown' into a world not of our own choosing and challenged to respond to the 'Call of Conscience' – to authentically engage with what it is 'to be.'

Existential philosophy offers a radically different perspective on who we are as individuals. To grasp the concept is to recognise its implications for individual choice and action. It considers the thinking, feeling, acting, and living human being, and considers us in terms of our own existence. In doing this, we are observed as individuals; the Self, and compared with other Selves; other individual people with whom we may interact.

The search for identity and the nature of Self has occupied poets, theologians, philosophers, psychologists and individuals for centuries. Psychotherapists and psychologists attempt to define the nature of who we are, and several perspectives on identity and self suggest that whilst interpersonal relationships are important, the Self is in some sense fixed and definable from the Selves of Others:

- Culture-pattern and Interpersonal Theorists point to the interpersonal nature of individual identity.
- Symbolic Interactionists assume that identity arises from our own interpretations of our social intercourse with others, and that we come to know who we are by seeing what others make of us.
- The Existential-Phenomenological (E-P) perspective questions the assumption of fixed identity, instead, seeing Self as a focal point 'in relation.' I.e. The-self-in-relation to others or to itself, rather than a fixed or separate entity.

The Self

The Self is not a substance but a verb, a potentiality. It is indefinable other than in a relational sense, meaning it is a relational construct (in relation to itself or other Selves) and the fixed notion of Self is a personally and culturally sedimented belief. *Sedimentation* is the term used to describe how our values and beliefs are 'sedimented' into our psyche from birth. If you think of how sediment builds up gradually over many years in the bed of a river, so it is with how our values are gradually absorbed into our sense of self from our family, our peers and our community. Often this has happened so slowly and insidiously that we are not aware of the difference between values that have been sedimented within us and values that we have consciously chosen for ourselves.

An alternative way of understanding the Self and accounting for unconscious phenomena (sedimented beliefs) is to distinguish between individuals developing their own invented or constructed sense of self (the believed-in Self), and those who develop their sense of self from the actuality of their lived experiences. The existentialists Spinelli and Alder both argue that we tend to disown or dissociate from those experiences that do not fit in with the believed-in self, either now or in the future. Instead of looking to the past to explain one's current sense of identity, Spinelli suggests that the past is a function of how an individual views themselves in the present, or how they imagine they would like to be or avoid being in the future.

Spinelli speaks of the Self and Other, explaining that our sense of separation and aloneness is due to us as humans creating a distinction between the two. At some point in our early development, each of us becomes 'self aware.' However, this requires us to make ourselves 'meaningful' by distinguishing that which is 'I' from that which is 'not I,' noting that our definitions are subject to our own interpretations. Therefore, if I see myself as having fixed characteristics which make up my identity – common in empirical psychological theory – contrary experiences force me to challenge this and expand the meaning I have given myself.

I can choose to accept this new view of myself and extend my meaning of myself, or reject and disown this to maintain a fixed meaning. If I accept this new, expanded view of myself, it shows that I am flexible and adaptable. It also infers greater meaninglessness, as the Self is now open to interpretation and I must question all prior beliefs. If I refuse to integrate this new understanding into my notion of Self, I am deceiving myself into believing that my fixed characteristics are all I am. In other words, 'I pretend to not experience that which I do experience.' Thus, I have choice over who I am becoming. I can choose to become more authentic through ownership of my experience, or maintain a sedimented self-structure.

Each has a cost, implying the existential notion of anxiety. If I accept I am a changing structure, I become anxious in my nothingness. If I refuse to evolve and change, I limit my potential to be something else; split off and prone to experiencing existential guilt. As Sartre said, 'We are condemned to choose.'[38] If I deceive myself, it creates a conflict between my current self-construct (understood to exist in terms of sedimented assumptions) and the currently experienced self- construct (without the imposition of those sedimented beliefs.)

Coming at it from this angle, it shows how the concept of 'Self' and 'Others' is constructed. This is in contrast to the concept of Self as fixed, and how it relates to other Selves, who are also fixed. In this way, the individual 'becomes' their Self through interdependent relationship: we create each other through our interactions and beliefs. This implies choice, and authentic or inauthentic modes of being.

Authenticity, according to Heidegger, refers to a way of being which engages with its possibilities and chooses its own way. Thus, authenticity is not about being different from the crowd and rejecting social mores or conventions, it is about knowingly choosing who we are against the backcloth of our very existence. To understand authenticity, one must grasp the concept of *Dasein* or 'being there.' This always means in relationship and never in isolation, i.e. *Mitsein*; 'Being-in-the-world-with-others.' Some psychological approaches assume that an individual's sense of being is continually created through interaction with the world. *Dasein* considers that an individual is 'not a substance with an essential nature and with properties or "accidents".' Rather, the possibility or potential of *Dasein* is the concept that it is not a definite, actual thing, but rather a possibility of various ways of being. In other words, we can choose who to be, and there are no limits to these choices.

They: Being Thrown into Circumstance

Despite *Dasein's* potentialities and possibilities of being, there are limits on its existence. Central to this concept is 'Thrown-ness.' The concept of Thrown-ness suggests that we are born into a world which we have not chosen: our family, culture, gender, and unique circumstances. It illuminates authentic and inauthentic modes of being: We are thrown into a world, shared with others, which contains expectations and social conventions, together with responses to it. We cannot choose the circumstances of our birth: the timing, zeitgeist, culture, parents etc. Our perception of others' expectations and social conventions constitutes 'They.' By responding to a way of being portrayed by '*They*' (known as '*Das Man*') we are living inauthentically and do not consider the possibility of other ways of being, or the various options for responding to life's challenges. Despite *Dasein's* capacity and potentiality for being open to its own Being, it often finds aspects of human existence threatening, puzzling or uncontrollable, and cuts itself off from those aspects of its Being. Such inauthenticity is a common state with Heidegger, who says: 'The Self of everyday *Dasein* is the they-self, which we distinguish from the authentic *Dasein*, is inauthentic insofar as it does things simply because that is what one does. It is authentic insofar as it makes up its own mind, is its own person or true to its own self.'[39]

Authenticity is not about genuineness or being real, nor is inauthenticity about being false. To dictate what is 'real' would contradict Heidegger's philosophy, as it would introduce a normative assessment of a right or proper way to be. However, after being thrown, *Dasein* has choices over 'how' it wants to be. 'The authentic person...has a constant awareness of the possibility of his own death; he is anxious, though not fearful, in the face of it. He sees his situation and the possibilities it presents to him, and makes a decision among them, in the light of this awareness.'

May describes non-being as an inseparable part of being. Whilst authentic existence requires an awareness of our ultimate non-being (that of death), the individual is faced with less dramatic but persistent loss of potentialities in conformism or absorption within society/They; *Das Man*. Conforming to the perceived norm resists anxiety, but at the cost of forfeiting our sense of mastery in choosing how to be. The family into which we are thrown, the culture into which we are born, and our unique life circumstances influence our construction of Self. The individual can decide to attribute their being to the expectations and developmental forces of others, or take responsibility for the choice to be who they are now and in the future.

Many existential writers have focused specifically on the family's role in determining our identity . The existential-phenomenological perspective considers how the family, as an agency of society, constitutes the 'Thrown-ness' of an individual's life. Other factors that might constitute 'Thrown-ness' include culture, gender, historical context, or child-rearing practice. However, instead of the person being a victim of their circumstances of birth and upbringing, this perspective suggests a greater sense of agency and choice in who one wants to become.

Modern Relevance of Existentialism

How can existential philosophy be of relevance to us in the 21st century and more particularly to choosing how we can live our lives meaningfully and enjoyably? In order to answer that question, it is useful to examine a number of existential themes, for example:

- Freedom and choice
- Anxiety
- Responsibility
- Authenticity
- Ultimate concerns

These are words used in our everyday language but with different existential meanings. How can we grasp their existential meaning when the original writings are often inaccessible?

In the previous chapters I have tried to interpret these concepts in a straightforward and accessible manner through the language of Myths. Through practical activities in the book, levelled at our individual everyday choices, we can explore our options, the implications of taking different paths and the anxiety that results from choosing.

For many of us, the concept of Myths has mystical connotations and is understood in an allegorical, legendary or fabled manner. I offer Myths differently as unquestioned assumptions that impinge on every aspect of our decision-making. Myths are therefore pervasive, fictitious, invented, make-believe or untrue. Within our social and cultural world we are bombarded with expectations and pressures of how to dress, what to eat, what career to pursue, or how to relate to other people. We are constantly told what to expect as we enter different life stages, as if each of us were no more than members of a cloned group. We can of course, choose how to respond to those expectations. We can conform, withdraw, or act as individuals or institutions to bring about social change. However, those unquestioned assumptions are so pervasive that we may never stand back from their stronghold and consider our choices beyond a narrowly defined set of options. Our culture and socialisation inhibits us exploring the vast array of available options. As Rousseau said, 'Man is born free but is everywhere in chains.'[40]

The existential meanings of choice, freedom, anxiety, responsibility and authenticity require interpretation at a level which makes sense in our everyday lives. Eight Myths were discussed in this book, together with the existential themes they suggest, namely:

- **The Identity Myth** — You're not good enough as you are and you should fit in with others' expectations and be someone other than who you want to be.
- **The Selfishness Myth** — You are selfish if you put your own needs before those of others.
- **The Group Myth** — It is better to be part of a group than be an individual.
- **The Commitment Myth** — You can't change things in your life once you have committed to them.
- **The Certainty Myth** — There are certain things in life that are fixed and solid and can always be relied on.
- **The Morality Myth** — There is an unquestionable moral code I should live my life by.
- **The Dishonesty Myth** — I should be discreet and modest in all my interactions rather than honest.
- **The Myth that You Can't Change** — Earlier choices in my life mean that future change is not an option.

Each of these Myths, and others, impinge on our everyday lives and limit our choices. Some are contentious and possibly provoke strong reactions in the reader.

The two central themes underlying these Myths are Freedom and Choice. By engaging with our freedom and realising our choices, anxiety and responsibility arise. Faced with the ultimate concern of our death, our limited time on this earth means we have to make choices and we never know the rightness of those choices – especially if we accept that no moral code exists in its ultimate form.

A central theme in existential philosophy is that there is no objective reality into which we are born and which exists separate from ourselves . We lull ourselves into a belief that we are not free and therefore unable to create who we want to be, allowing our social and cultural Myths to dictate the reality of our lives. Sartre says we act in Bad Faith in an attempt to fool ourselves that we are not free . We attempt to build numerous structures through roles, norms, cultures, and beliefs to define our sense of reality – to give the illusion that a blueprint exists into which we fit and are part of. As Van Deurzen-Smith says, 'It is the basic skill of fooling oneself, of rocking oneself to sleep, of contenting oneself with illusions; the basic human accomplishment of self-deception; bad faith or *mauvaise foi*.'[41]

Affecting Change in Others

How can existential philosophy be of relevance to us in helping others to change? It begins with recognising where we are still abiding by the Myths of our own lives.

Knowing we have choices, we must learn to live with the anxiety of challenging the status quo, or questioning the rightness of our own decisions. We may have already dealt with this anxiety by choosing to go vegan, relinquishing a religion, or challenging a widely-held belief that you have discovered is fallible. And despite knowing that feeling of anxiety, we are still bound by our own Myths. We have to live in the social world and consider others and the rules which enable us to realise our choices. The issue is not one of rejecting all that is expected of us – the issue is that we do have a choice. The question is whether we challenge the unquestioned assumptions, expand our choices and live with the anxiety that meaningful living entails.

Understanding this gives us a deeper insight into why others around us resist change. If we as 'enlightened' beings are still subject to these Myths, then it's easy to see how those still bound by all those social norms are even more deeply entrenched in their beliefs and habits.

We are constantly bombarded with choices about how to live and how to be happy, and when our choices logically change, based on newfound information, we expect that others will follow suit, once shown the same information. The physical and emotional anxiety that results from others not changing can be likened to the anxiety the other person may experience when presented with that new information. All of a sudden, everything they knew and believed in is in question. They may feel lied to, judged, shamed, or any other number of emotions. Moving away from that anxiety means denying the Self - denying growth through new information and evolution of the Self. However, it also means a recognisable safety, staying within the bubble of sedimented beliefs.

Think for a moment about how Myths function in your own life. Society's Myths often result in us choosing from a limited array of available options – it is assumed that 'having it all but in balance' is the way forward. Knowing that, even with an open mind, you are still living with Myths, it becomes easier to sympathise with those who have never even considered that they have choices in life.

As a psychotherapist, I passionately believe that we are each the best judge of what is right for us. By examining the role of Myths in our lives, we can expand our options, reconnect with our choices and judge the rightness of them. By recognising the role of Myths in other people's lives, we can help to gently open their eyes by encouraging them to question, rather than forcing a viewpoint on them or arguing with someone who is not yet ready to take on new information.

Change at any level brings anxiety, particularly where a deep-rooted belief is challenged. Resistance is almost inevitable, as the individual grapples with new knowledge versus what they 'know.' Recognise that people deal with this anxiety in different ways, some coming about change sooner than others. Be patient, and use your own experience as a mirror and a guide to slowly steer them towards recognising the power and freedom of choice in their life.

If our Selves truly are developed through our interactions with others, we can use our heightened sense of Self to help others learn and grow. We have the power and the freedom to do so.

References

1 May, R. (1975:12) *The Courage To Create*. UK. Norton Co. Inc.

2 Laing. R.D. (1970:58) *The Politics of Experience*. NY: Ballantine Books

3, ibid. 1.

4 ibid. 1

5 Sartre, J.P. (1948:40) *Existentialism and Humanism*. London: Methuen Publishing Limited

6 Heidegger, M. (1962:155) *Being and Time*. US: Harper & Row Publishers Inc.

7 ibid. 6, 343

8 Cohn, H.W. (2002:89) *Heidegger and the roots of Existential Therapy*. UK: Continuum

9. Cooper, D. (1972:11) *The Death of the Family*. 2nd edn. UK: Pelican,

10. Janis, J.L. (1982) *Victims of Groupthink*. 2nd edn. US: Houghton

11. ibid. 8

12. ibid. 8, 98

13. Kierkegaard, S. (1992:10) *Either/Or. A Fragment of Life*. (trans) Alastair Hannnay: UK

14. Van-Deurzen, E. (1988:38) *Existential Counselling in Practice*. UK: Sage Publications

15. Morgan, G. (1986:212-3) *Images of Organization*. UK: Sage Publications Inc.

16. ibid. 14, 38

17. ibid. 14, 43

18. ibid. 14

19. Binswanger, L. (1946) *'The existential analysis school of thought', in Existence*. (eds) R.May, E. Angel, & H.F. Ellenberger. New York: Basic Books 1958

20. Boss, M. (1963) *Psychoanalysis and Daseinanalysis*. (trans) I.B. Lefebre. New York: Basic Books

21. ibid. 5

22. ibid. 5, 30

23. ibid. 13
24. Kierkegaard, S. (1980:10) *The Sickness Unto Death: A Christian Psychological Exposition for Upbuilding and Awakening*. vol. 19, (trans) H.V. Hong and E.H. Hong. Princeton, NJ: Princeton University Press. (Original work published 1849)
25. Sartre, J.P. (1948:27) *Existentialism and Humanism*. London: Methuen Publishing Limited
26. ibid. 25, 30
27. ibid. 25, 33
28. ibid. 25, 39
29. ibid. 25, 40
30. Murdoch, I. (2001) *The Sea, The Sea*. Penguin Classics;
31. Miller, A. (1994) *For Your Own Good: The Roots Of Violence In Child-Rearing*. UK: Virago
32. ibid. 31, 27
33. Winnicott, D. W. (1965) *The Family and Individual Development*. New York
34. Spinelli, E. (1999) 'The Interpreted World'. An Introduction to Phenomenological Psychology. UK: Sage Publications.
35. Van-Deurzen-Smith, E. (1998:59) *Paradox and Passion in Psychotherapy: An Existential Approach to Therapy and Counselling*. Chichester: Wiley
36. Mann, C. (2013) *Communicate: How to say what needs to be said, when it needs to be said, in the way it needs to be said*. Australia: Communicate31
37. Nietzsche,F. (1883) Thus Spake Zarathustra. R.J. Hollingdale. Harmondsworth: Penguin 1961
38. Sartre, J.P. (1946) *Existentialism and Humanism*. London: Methuen Publishing Limited
39. ibid. 6, 167
40. Rousseau, J.J. (1968:49) *The Social Contract*. Penguin Classics
41. Van Deurzen-Smith, E. (1997) *Everyday Mysteries: Existential Dimensions of Psychotherapy*. UK: Routledge

Appendix

Download a printable version of this exercise from
https://communicate31.com/168hours

Day

	6-7am	7-8am	8-9am	9-10am	10-11am	11-12pm	12-1pm	1-2pm	2-3pm	3-4pm	4-5pm	5-6pm
Mon												
Tue												
Wed												
Thu												
Fri												
Sat												
Sun												

Night

	6-7pm	7-8pm	8-9pm	9-10pm	10-11pm	11-12am	12-1am	1-2am	2-3am	3-4am	4-5am	5-6am
Mon												
Tue												
Wed												
Thu												
Fri												
Sat												
Sun												

About Clare Mann

BSc (Hons) MSc MA Post Grad Dip. C,Occ Psychol. FBPS AMAPS

Clare Mann is an Australian-based psychologist, existential psychotherapist, best-selling author, speaker and communications trainer. She runs public and in-house training programs in communication, team-building and ethical leadership, and regularly appears on TV and in the press. She has authored and contributed to numerous books. One of her books, Communicate, has international acclaim with the foreword written by US presidential advisor Doug Wead. She was awarded Fellowships in both the British Psychological Society and the Australian Human Resources Institute for her contribution to these professions.

Clare believes that, at this time in our history, we are facing enormous ethical, social, environmental, and existential challenges and that social justice activists are the harbingers of a new dawn of consciousness. She seeks ways to help people embrace new ways of thinking, and helps reduce individual and institutionalised resistance to ideas outside of the mainstream. Her expertise in uncovering myths, coupled with developing a person's linguistic skills helps individuals break the impasse and address these social and ethical concerns.

Clare is an ethical vegan and the author of Vystopia: The Anguish of Being Vegan in a Non-Vegan World. She provides face-to-face and online skills training to help vegans and social justice advocates communicate and collaborate more effectively.